Ewald Eisen

**We all look for new ways to
lead a healthier lifestyle and to
improve our overall well-being.
Let's not make the mistake to limit our
focus on nutrition and physical activity.**

What we forget to keep in mind is that our body needs one thing first and foremost to live: Water. We all know that the human body is made up primarily of water. Water is the elixir of life, and our most valuable natural resource. Nothing impacts our well-being more than the quality of the water we drink.

Every day, we can make a choice to drink processed, "dead" water or to drink fresh, lively water, that's full of energy. This book explores a natural way to create vital water. Crystal water.

Water is not just an assembly of oxygen and hydrogen molecules. It's not just H_2O. Scientists discovered that water has a memory and that it can be positively stimulated by sources of vibration and energy. Sources like gemstones.

Water and stones – this combination has accompanied me throughout a healthy and active life for more than 30 years. After all these years, I have come to this conclusion:

You can't reinvent water. Just the way you drink it!

CONTENTS

Preface: The Laws of Nature 8

Thank you 12

The miracles of nature 14

Water and stones 22

WATER

Water, the most extraordinary element 26

Global water shortage 34

Water and climate 40

Different types of drinking water 44

Living water - healthy water 52

When is water healthy and safe? 58

Methods to improve your drinking water's quality at home 64

Institutes for water analysis 72

Influental water researchers 74

Masaru Emoto 77

Dr. Fereydoon Batmanghelidj 83

Water provides for a healthy body 86

Water - a blessing for our body 90

Rules for drinking 101

Water and awareness 104

Sobonfu Somé 108

CRYSTALS

Stones - primal element of nature 116

The 85 most important healing crystals 124

Helpful gemstones - Physical 213

Helpful gemstones - Mental 217

CRYSTAL WATER

The largest water treatment on earth 222

Crystal water - a new opportunity for our health 227

Laboratory results on crystal water 232

Wine and gemstones 236

Plants and crystal water 240

The "seventh sense" of animals 244

Preparation of crystal water 248

Application symbols 258

Chakra energy centers 258

Special crystal water recipes 260

Individual crystal water 286

Gemstone blends for INU bottles 290

Crystal water - the drink of the future 298

Dr. Peter Kastner, Dr. Gabnus Iheanacho Okafor 300

Summary 302

Sources 306

GEMSTONE DIRECTORY

Agate	128	Dolomite	150
Amazonite	129	Dumortierite	151
Amber	130	Emerald	152
Amethyst	131	Epidote	153
Ametrine	132	Fire opal	154
Angelite	133	Fluorite	155
Apatite	134	Fuchsite	156
Aquamarine	135	Garnet	157
Aventurine	136	Halite	158
Azurite	137	Howlite	159
Bloodstone (Hematite)	138	Jade	160
Calcite	139	Jasper, Red	161
Carnelian	140	Jet	162
Celestine	141	Kunzite	163
Chalcedony	142	Labradorite	164
Chrysocolla	143	Lapis lazuli	165
Chrysoprase	144	Larimar	166
Citrine	145	Lemon calcite	167
Clear Quartz	146	Leopard jasper	168
Coral	147	Lepidolite	169
Diamond	148	Magnesite	170
Disthene	149	Magnetite	171

Malachite 172

Milk opal 173

Moldavite 174

Mookaite 175

Moonstone 176

Morganite 177

Moss agate 178

Nephrite 179

Obsidian 180

Ocean agate 181

Onyx 182

Opal 183

Peridot 184

Petrified wood 185

Pearl 186

Pyrite 187

Rainbow obsidian 188

Rhodochrosite 189

Rhodonite 190

Rose Quartz 191

Ruby 192

Rutile Quartz 193

Sapphire 194

Selenite 195

Serpentine 196

Shungite 197

Smoky Quartz 198

Sodalite 199

Sugilite 200

Sunstone 201

Tanzanite 202

Tiger's Eye 203

Topaz 204

Tourmaline, Black 205

Tourmaline, Green 206

Tourmaline, Pink 207

Tourmaline, Red 208

Tourmaline, Watermelon . 209

Turquoise 210

Zircon 211

Zoisite 212

PREAMBLE
THE LAWS OF NATURE

We live on the most magnificent planets in our universe, our "MOTHER EARTH". There is certainly not a more appropriate term for our planet than "MOTHER", because nothing is associated more with one's mother than care - affection - love - healing - security - trust - compassion.

Similarly, we associate the same characterization with nature.

- She provides for a healthy climate and sufficient oxygen
- She produces all the medicinal herbs and plants for our health
- We live in abundance because plants are always producing new seeds for fruits.
- She offers us security for a carefree life.
- Everything seems to work by itself, because the laws of our nature are so ingeniously coordinated and interact brilliantly.

We live on this planet together with Mother Nature and all her irrefutable rules that by themselves provide for a perfect, harmonious co-existence and a wonderful life. In our times, most actions and decisions humans make are not in accordance with the rules of nature anymore. They contradict with those universal laws.

And of course nature reacts to those actions. And those reactions threaten our existence. Climate change is the best example. With our greed and carelessness we threaten nature's balance. And that imbalance causes countless catastrophes already. Another example is the amount of areas that are sealed by roads, buildings and other human infrastructure. Those sealed areas already make up about 20.9% of our planet. This has the effect that water cannot properly seep away into the ground anymore, thus disturbing the natural cycle of water. When water doesn't seep into the ground but is washed into a sewer, it won't be cleaned and revitalized naturally, but is mixed with poisons and has to be artificially cleaned in treatment plants. You can imagine what that does to the quality of your water.

Of course, you can question every rule and phenomenon of nature. You can try to measure and analyze every little bit of nature's secrets. But what you'll find is that those rules are made up very simply and genially, controlling all life on earth.

In our lives, we are given countless choices. There's one choice that we're not given, though: to act against the laws of nature. This is why acting in accordance with those rules is a principle I very much recommend.

In this book I will discuss very intensively the two primal elements, water and stones, because the more we know about these essential elements, the better! We can use them for ourselves. With the natural power of water and stones, we can enjoy our lives to the fullest and look forward to a long, active life.

THE MOST SIGNIFICANT ELEMENTS OF NATURE ARE WATER AND STONE.

> „*The greatest wonder that exists is the world - go and discover it.*“
>
> — Kurt Tucholsky

THANK YOU

Since the age of 20, I have strived to always drink the healthiest water available. Throughout this period, until today, I have met many people who had a similar motivation. Often friends, but also scientists who were decidedly engaged in the subject of water. I attended seminars, congresses and lectures and read many books on the subject. I was able to learn from all of them. For this I would like to thank them very much.

On this path I also began to develop my passion for stones. On this journey I met wonderful people, warm-hearted, with a very deep knowledge of one of our most important natural elements. I would also like to thank these friends for the countless hours in which they taught me many things about stones and their effects.

Last but not least, I want to thank my family, who now shares my passion as intensely as I do.

To all my deepest, heartfelt thanks

Ewald Eisen

THE MIRACLES
OF NATURE

Nowadays, we are fascinated by the constant inventions and achievements in digital life. Artificial intelligence is the driving force of our new age: billions of computerized processes in a matter of seconds, algorithms that follow intelligent rules, millions of links from individual scientific findings to the network of a modern perfection. Nevertheless, our great science is far from having explored all the innumerable phenomena of our nature or even from having replaced them with man-made software.

The miracle of nature is exemplified in a simple question: How does a tulip bulb know that it is supposed to sprout, grow and bloom in early March?

In addition to external factors such as length of day and ambient temperature, internal factors such as plant hormones, genes, can also influence whether and when a plant flowers. Many plants even have a kind of internal warmth counter: they can add up warm days and thus determine quite accurately whether the time for growth has arrived. Only when a certain number of warmer days have passed, the bushes begin to sprout.

This example shows us what sophisticated rules and signals nature has established even for a simple plant. Consequently, how complex must be the interactions of millions of dependencies in us highly developed living beings?

The biodiversity of our planet is infinite. It is assumed there is a diversity of almost nine million animal and plant species.

Just under three-quarters of these are land creatures, and a good quarter are sea creatures. No computer, no software comes close to being able to map such complex dependencies. All the millions of species live in a balanced coexistence that allows each species its niche and its place. From this we see the brilliance of nature.

Nevertheless, we take nature for granted and give little thought to the connections and complicated interdependencies that determine our lives. Yet, in fact, it is essential for survival to recognize the laws of nature and live by them. Any disregard inevitably leads to momentous changes, albeit over a long period of time.

No one can deny that man has already disregarded nature to the point of destruction: The explosion of nuclear power plants, oil spills on all the world's oceans, the increasingly severe droughts caused by climate change speak a clear language. We should be well aware: at the end of the day, we are guests on earth. Nature is always "in the driver's seat" because we are fully dependent on it.

However, if we live in harmony with our Mother Earth and treat it with care, that is our guarantee for a healthy and happy life - and also for the many generations that will come after us.

NATURE DOES NOT TOLERATE VIOLATIONS OF ITS LAWS.

On our planet we are fascinated by gigantic natural phenomena such as:

- Geysers
- Aurora Borealis & Aurora Australis
- Volcanism
- Marine phosphorescence
- Perito Moreno Glacier
- Mysterious light pillars in Canada
- Cueva de los Cristales (Cave of Crystals) from Chihuahua
- and many more

THE TREASURES OF NATURE CONTAIN COUNTLESS APPS.

But it is the unseen wonders that we take for granted that make our nature so colossal. This includes how water absorbs and stores information, how the assembly of water and oxygen molecules transmits information that can make you healthy or sick. In this way, the water, influenced by stones, has a powerful impact on our body. It fascinates me how the formation of stones is decisive for their effect on humans, how stones influence, impair or enrich their environment and thereby our lives via electromagnetic frequencies.

Smartphones and the countless apps impact our daily lives. Apps can quickly give us important information, help us get better organized, support us in many areas of life, count steps or calories, make suggestions about our diet and health, and much more. However, nature for thousands of years has been providing us with millions of apps that make our lives more livable.

Here are a few examples.

Did you know ...

... that a stinging nettle app:

- cleanses the blood, staunches bleeding
- and promotes blood formation improves our metabolism
- cures urinary tract diseases, relieves rheumatism and gout, treats loss of appetite
- cures diarrhea
- supports the healing of stomach and kidney weakness, alleviates high blood pressure
- relieves menstrual cramps

... that a cumin app:

- has an antibacterial effect
- stimulates appetite
- has an antibacterial effect
- curbs flatulence
- promotes blood circulation
- is germ-inhibiting
- has a digestive effect
- is refreshing and fungicidal

... that a rosemary app:

- is antibacterial, relaxing, antispasmodic
- kills fungi and inhibits inflammation
- has analgesic properties
- relieves respiratory problems
- curbs diarrhea
- relieves rheumatism and gout
- relieves headaches and migraines
- acts against nervous restlessness and states of exhaustion
- cures persistent skin rashes, eczema and hemorrhoids
- eliminates flatulence and indigestion
- treats low blood pressure, nervous heart complaints and cardiac insufficiency

... that an aquamarine app:

- has a positive effect on the body and psyche
- relieves asthma
- strengthens the eyesight
- promotes concentration
- prevents signs of aging
- strengthens the immune system and endurance
- has a positive effect on the thyroid gland and regulates the hormonal balance
- is helpful with allergies and strengthens the respiratory system, relieves depression and weather sensitivity

Did you know ...

... that a clear quartz app:

- relieves physical pain and discomfort of a general natureworks against dizziness
- dampens nervousness and tensionalleviates weather sensitivity
- treats stomach and intestinal problems successfullyhelps women especially during menopause
- Animals respond particularly well to gemstone therapy with clear quartz.

The Abbess Hildegard von Bingen (1098-1179) successfully applied and documented the effects of crystals and herbs in numerous treatments almost a thousand years ago.

All of her writings are as relevant today as they were then. Here is an excerpt from her work on clear quartz:

„If your eyes get weak, warm a crystal in the sun and then put it on your eyes. This pulls the bad juices out of the eyes and the person gets his sight back. Those who have swollen glands on the neck should warm a crystal in the sun and then bind it to the glands day and night. He should proceed in this way regularly until the swellings disappear. If one has a stomach ache, stomach trouble, or heart trouble, heat a clear quartz in the sun and pour water over it. Subsequently, he puts the crystal in this water for an hour, then takes it out again and drinks from it regularly until he gets better.“

THUS, THE DIVERSITY OF "NATURE'S APPS" ILLUSTRATES THE AMAZING WEALTH THAT OUR NATURAL ENVIRONMENT CONSTANTLY HOLDS IN STORE.

> *„Everything that nature itself orders is good for some purpose. The entire nature in general is actually nothing else than a connection of phenomena according to rules and there is no Randomness anywhere.“*
>
> — Immanuel Kant

WATER AND
STONES

WATER

the most extraordinary element

24

Water is the most valuable element that Earth has to offer. Without water, humans, plants and animals would not survive and our green-blue planet would not exist. Without water, Earth would be a dusty, lifeless planet like many others in our universe that we have discovered so far.

Water is the only chemical compound on Earth that occurs naturally as a liquid, a solid, and a gas. The term water is used for the liquid state of aggregation. In the solid state we refer to ice, in the gaseous state to vapor.

When astronomers search the universe for planets where life would be possible, they always start by analyzing if that planet has signs of water. It is the only element that higher developed organisms need without any alternative. Water is elementary for life, growth and preservation of species on Earth.

Water cannot be produced or duplicated: We have always been drinking the same water since the beginning of time.

STONES
primal force of our planet

Stone - this is the name given to the solid, inanimate component of Earth's crust. The Formation of stone takes a lot of time - sometimes millions of years! Stone consists mainly of so-called minerals, individual elements or chemical compounds that have changed as a result of geological processes. In terms of color and size, the variety is enormous: depending on how resistant they are and how much they have been worked by wind, water and other factors, stones can take on all the colors of the rainbow. Their shape also ranges from fissured to cubic to amorphous. Various processes are likely to be responsible for the formation of the different stone types: sometimes their origin goes back to a volcanic eruption, other stones were formed in the water - more precisely by minerals, but also remains of plants and animals as well as other suspended matter being deposited on top of each other at the bottom of the sea. In the course of time, several such layers have been deposited on top of each other and have been pressed together more and more tightly. These layers were formed 150 to 250 million years ago, while other types of stone were formed by transformation processes - for example, under high pressure and high temperatures in the interior of Earth's crust.

WATER
THE MOST
EXTRAORDINARY
ELEMENT

The properties of water have fundamental meanings for life on Earth.

Its physical, chemical properties are based on the structure of the water molecule and the resulting chains and interactions of the water molecules with each other. The two elements in water are hydrogen and oxygen. They form compounds, known as molecular clusters, with the help of electrical dipole forces. These irregularly arranged bundles of molecules form depending on what information the water is receiving or fetching at that moment.

In nature, water does not occur as a pure substance, it practically always contains dissolved substances (mainly ions of salts), although possibly in hardly measurable concentrations. Such dissolved substances change the properties of the water.

WE HAVE BEEN DRINKING THE SAME WATER FOR THOUSANDS OF YEARS.

The origin of water on Earth, in particular the question of why there is significantly more water on Earth than on other planets, has not been adequately clarified yet. Part of the water undoubtedly entered the atmosphere through the outgassing of magma, so it ultimately came from Earth's interior. However, whether this can explain the amount of water is highly doubted. The element hydrogen is the most abundant element in the universe, and oxygen also occurs in large quantities, but usually bound in silicates and metal oxides.

As in the human body, the dominant portion of Earth's surface (70 percent) is covered by water. Earth's water resources amount to approximately 1.4 billion cubic kilometers, of which the vast majority is salt water from the oceans. Only 48 million cubic kilometers (3.5 percent) of Earth's water exists as fresh water.

WATER COMES FROM INSIDE THE EARTH.

The distribution of water on our planet is divided as follows:

Oceans .... 83.51 %
Non-extractable groundwater (too deep) .... 15.45 %
Polar ice .... 1.007 %
Rivers .... 0.015 %
Extractable groundwater .... 0.015 %
Atmosphere .... 0.0008 %

Accordingly, only 0.03 percent is available as fresh water, so the available drinking water reserves are very limited. In purely mathematical terms, there are 495 quadrillion (that's 495 with 15 zeros!) liters worldwide that could be used as drinking water. This amount neither increases nor decreases: water is not consumed, but is in circulation and is always recycled.

Earth's water cycle keeps water on our planet: Used water flows in rivers to the sea and through evaporation becomes clouds. It returns to the ground as rain, which again forms new groundwater and feeds rivers and lakes. There is really no such thing as "new water". Since the existence of humankind, we always drink the same water.

WE ALSO STILL ENJOY THE WATER THAT JESUS CHRIST TURNED INTO WINE AT A WEDDING MORE THAN 2000 YEARS AGO.

The natural cycle of water shows once more how brilliantly "Mother Nature" ensures our life on Earth. Water that we drink daily and excrete through the body, including that which we need for hygiene, flows back into this great cycle. Water from industrial use, heavily contaminated, is also recycled.

In principle, all the water we use is contaminated: by toxins and chemicals from industry or residues of medicines and personal care products that dissolve into the water. These dissolved contaminants must be separated from clear water again. This is done by wastewater treatment plants in each municipality that recycles water.

However, by far the world's largest recycler of water is Nature. She regenerates water through the global water cycle:

- Contaminated water evaporates and forms clouds.
- Clouds will rain down to the ground.
- The water trickles into the earth.
- There are billions of tons of stones in the earth.
- Stones regenerate our water completely and energetically.

At springs, the water emerges healthy and full of energy again. Or it accumulates in ground water reservoirs, where it is available to us again.

NATURE IS THE WORLD'S LARGEST WATER TREATMENT PLANT.

Responsible for the weather, whether we are happy about it or complain about it, is the water cycle. What can we learn from this?

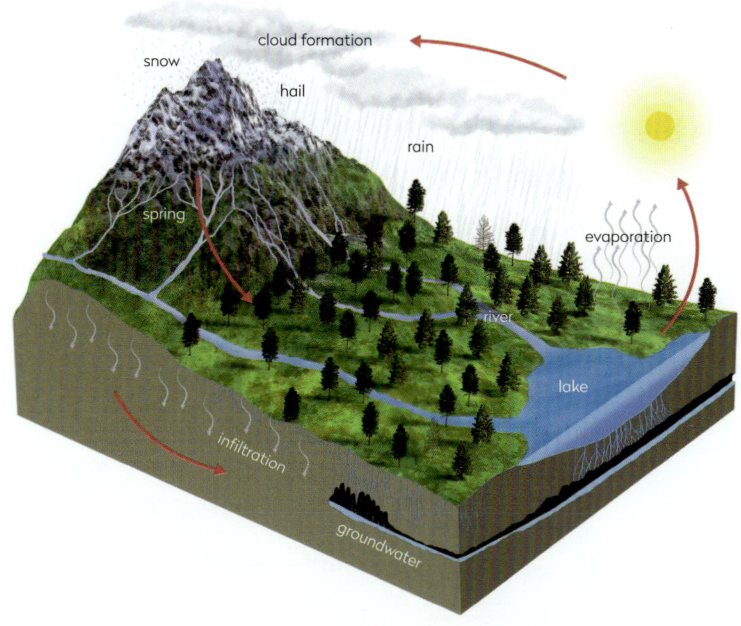

Each country provides drinking water for the use of its citizens. It comes partly from rain water, surface water in rivers, lakes, from groundwater reservoirs, mineral water and spring water. The use of water bodies is regulated by law. Central Europe has a reliable, mainly cost-covering and high-quality drinking water supply. This water is mostly provided by public suppliers (municipal suppliers) who take the ecological responsibility and provide it as tap water.

The global water market is growing faster than almost any other industry. Therefore, private suppliers have a great interest in exploiting water as a commodity. The insufficient supply of a large part of the world's population with hygienic and toxicologically safe drinking water as well as a sufficient amount of usable water is one of the greatest challenges for mankind in the coming decades. Since 1990, around 2.6 billion more people have gained access to a safe water supply, for example with the help of wells or a pipeline system. But 663 million people still drink water that is polluted or contaminated every day, or have no access to water at all. For these people, especially for the children, this situation is health-threatening, even life-threatening.

Thousands of people suffer gruesome deaths every day, dying of thirst or becoming infected because they do not have access to healthy water.

THOUSANDS OF PEOPLE DIE EVERY DAY DUE TO LACK OF DRINKABLE WATER.

> *„Drinking water is essential
> to a healthy lifestyle."*
>
> — Stephen Curry

GLOBAL WATER
SHORTAGE

Most of Earth is covered with water, but only 0.3 percent of it is drinkable. This drinkable water is also very unevenly distributed. In Africa, Latin America and Asia in particular, there are dramatic water shortages in many places.

2.1 billion people have no access to clean water. And 884 million people do not have a basic supply of water.

Those most affected are families in the poorest regions of the world - especially in rural areas. But water must not only be clean, it must be "safe". UNICEF defines "safe" water as water that is accessible to people close to home, available when needed, and, of course, free of contamination. Only then can families be confident that their health is not at risk. What good is it if there is water nearby, but it comes from a polluted river and is full of pathogens?

WATER MUST NOT ONLY BE CLEAN, IT MUST BE SAFE.

Contaminated water is one problem - another one is the lack of hygiene. Around two billion people do not use safe sanitation. This includes, for example, a toilet that ensures that people do not come in contact with the excreta or that has a system in place to dispose of the excreta safely. Contact with pathogens in feces is the main cause of the high mortality rate in these regions - especially among children. South Sudan is a warning example here: a cholera outbreak claimed more than 400 lives since the summer of 2016.

Each year, more than 360,000 children die from preventable diarrheal diseases caused by contaminated water or poor sanitation.

WITHOUT WATER AND HYGIENE, DISEASES SPREAD PARTICULARLY QUICKLY.

Millions of people often haul a few gallons of water for hours to get a meager supply. Often, the only task of a day is to secure a family's need for drinking water. Try imagining the next time you drink a glass of water that you had to walk a whole day to get that glass. You will perceive each sip completely differently.

In many countries just north of the equator, water shortage is extremely high - affecting a quarter of the world's population. This applies especially to:

- North- and South Africa
- Saudi Arabia and neighboring small nations in the Sudan
- North and South America
- Afghanistan
- Kazakhstan Mongolia
- Parts of China and Korea
- Chile
- Iraq
- Iran

WATER SHORTAGES IN THE WORLD'S POOREST REGIONS SHOULD GIVE US A NEW AWARENESS OF WATER.

In these countries, 80 percent of available water resources are already consumed in a normal year. However, if a heat wave or prolonged drought happens, a dramatic water shortage looms with life-threatening consequences for humans and animals. This situation is so devastating that we need to develop a new attitude towards water. There are international organizations that provide enormous help to the people of the affected regions already and save many lives every day. Clean drinking water and hygiene are essential for survival - and often help to improve life as a whole: Because with their own well in the village, girls in particular have more time for school. Fetching water from distant sources often consumes a lot of their time and energy. UNICEF builds wells and repairs pipelines. In war and disaster areas, UNICEF supplies families with clean drinking water. If you would like to support people in water-scarce areas, please find here the donation address:

www.unicef.org

Viva con Agua - together with its project partners - has reached around three million people (as of April 2019) worldwide with WASH projects. This has provided them with access to clean drinking water, sanitation, hygiene facilities, as well as training and education. "Without wells, everything is nothing, but wells are not everything!" That is the organization's motto. It highlights importance of holistic project approaches that go beyond the mere provision of hardware (in addition to wells, toilets, hand-washing facilities, etc.) and helps to ensure that these facilities also function long term. The donation address:

www.vivaconagua.org

"Life needs Water" LNW e. V. is an international organization specializing in the construction of drinking water wells in water-scarce countries. The organization takes up the challenge to implement water projects with solar pumping systems in the areas where there is extreme water shortage. "When we show people how simple and sustainable access to water can be, it positively changes their lives. We motivate them to help others build better lives, too!" The donation address: **www.lifeneedswater.org**

In 2016, World Vision provided clean water to more than 4.6 million people through ist projects. Every ten seconds, a person thus gained access to clean drinking water. World Vision describes its work as follows: "Water harvesting is our most important area of work. Together with the native people, we drill or rehabilitate wells, build protected water intakes, collection tanks and filter systems. Training sessions teach people how to maintain pumps and wells." The donation address: **www.worldvision.de**

Having studied this subject in great detail, in my opinion these four organizations are so reputable that I myself also donate to them.

> *„Love alone understands the secret of giving*
> *to others while becoming rich oneself.“*
>
> — Clemens Brentano

THERE IS
NO
PLANET
B

WATER AND CLIMATE

There is a good reason why Earth is called the "Blue Planet". The water cycle is an important part of the climate system that makes life on Earth possible. Areas covered by water or ice, for example, reflect the sunrays and thus ensure that Earth's temperature remains at a comfortable level. Water vapor in the atmosphere also regulates temperature. And the Gulf Stream is the largest heating system for Europe: its water masses bring the warmth of the equator all the way up to Norway. In the form of rainfall, water is a special climate element, but it is very dependent on the prevailing temperature. If the earth warms only minimally, this will lead to increased evaporation of water on the world's oceans and thus to significantly higher rainfalls. Increased rainfall in the form of storms, heavy rain, snowfall, etc. is already dominating the global climate.

GLOBAL WARMING CAUSES WATER SHORTAGE.

Water is life - and essential for people, animals, plants, and any kind of social and economic development. Today, about four billion people suffer from severe water shortages for at least one month a year. The fact that every degree counts when it comes to global warming is confirmed by the Intergovernmental Panel on Climate Change's (IPCC) 2018 1.5-degree Special Report.

According to the report, the number of people suffering from additional water scarcity due to climate change is expected to double if the global temperature rises by two degrees Celsius.

By 2050, demand for water could increase by 55 percent, putting even more pressure on the resource. Cities will be particularly affected, as they will lack two-thirds of the water that is still available today.

At the same time, parts of Central America and Asia are already suffering from extremely heavy rainfall. Climate change will further worsen these problems in many places - whether through too much, too little, or polluted water.

However, the resource water itself also contributes to the emission of greenhouse gases. Treatment and distribution of drinking water and the treatment of wastewater requires a great deal of energy and releases large quantities of greenhouse gases. However, more energy-efficient supply networks and environmentally and climate-friendly handling of wastewater and sewage sludge can significantly limit carbon dioxide and methane emissions.

INTELLIGENT WATER TREATMENT PROTECTS THE CLIMATE.

Wetlands, which rely on a constant supply of clean water, are essential to preserve for climate protection: It is estimated that peatlands store twice as much carbon as all the world's forests combined.

However, water is not only drunk or needed for energy generation, water is also necessary in different industrial processes. Whether in agriculture or the energy industry, water is used here in enormous quantities – broken down, every person on Earth uses 185 gallons per day. That's the equivalent of five bathtubs for each person! This example shows how important it is to minimize the use of water. Every individual can make a contribution to this.

> „*The world needs decisive leadership*
> *to combat climate change.*"
> — Leonardo DiCaprio —

DIFFERENT TYPES
OF DRINKING WATER

Drinking water can come from groundwater, surface water, rainwater or ocean water. It can be drunk either untreated or after preparation, but it must meet the minimum hygienic and microbiological requirements. The limit values are specified in a drinking water ordinance with regard to undesirable substances such as lead, nitrite and sulfite. All drinking water should contain a minimum amount of minerals, but must not contain any harmful microorganisms.

Table water

Table water can be made from tap water or natural mineral water and must comply with drinking water guidelines. Imitation mixtures are also possible, for which tap water and other ingredients such as salt water or mineral water may be used. Table water may contain one or more of the following ingredients: Brine, salts or salt solutions, carbon dioxide. The content of dissolved solids must not exceed 2 g/l. If the carbon dioxide content exceeds 4 g/l, table water can also be referred to as soda water. It is not tied to a specific source and may be produced and bottled anywhere. Table water can be offered through taps and transported in larger containers. Unlike mineral water, it does not require official approval.

TABLE WATER DOES NOT REQUIRE OFFICIAL APPROVAL.

Mineral water

Natural mineral water typically originates from an underground, protected source and is of pristine purity. This must be microbiologically proven, chemically safe and nutritionally effective. Mineral water must be bottled either directly at the source or in the immediate vicinity. No other substances may be added, only the natural content of minerals is allowed. Many mineral molecules, however, are too large to pass through the cell membrane; they are held up in the cellular pre-tissue and tend to clog cellular access. Thus, the indications of proportions of minerals are not synonymous with a health effect. It may not be treated. If the natural content of carbon dioxide exceeds 250 mg/l, the officially recognized water from underground deposits is called acidulous water.

> **MINERAL WATER SPRINGS ARE ALWAYS LOCATED IN ROCKY AREAS.**

Tap water

The water from the tap is extracted and treated decentrally in a local waterworks from groundwater or surface water. The composition of tap water is constantly controlled, but differs from region to region. Values such as water hardness can be found on the Internet or obtained from the water supplier. Tap water distributors advertise with the slogan: "Tap water is the best controlled food, it is tested daily."

However, it is concealed that of 1700 dissolved substances in water only approx. 36 are tested, no drug residues, no hormones, etc. At the same time, the limits have been raised again and again in recent years so that they can be undercut.

The largest portion in drinking water reservoirs is "circulating water", i.e. water; which flows into the drain, is reprocessed in wastewater treatment plants and flows back into drinking water reservoirs. Rarely is it fresh water from a spring. It includes wastewater contaminated after domestic, commercial, industrial or agricultural use, i.e. wastewater from toilets, kitchens, clinics or businesses, as well as rainwater contaminated with dust or pollutants.

Particularly polluted industrial wastewater is usually treated or pre-treated in the company's own facilities. Wastewater treatment plants use biological and chemical treatment processes, including mechanical sediment filters that remove undissolved substances. Treatment with ozone and activated carbon has proven to be very effective. Experts say it is an illusion to believe that all substances in water can be detected, for the simple reason that new drugs are constantly being added. Problems are caused by high nitrate contamination in groundwater due to excessive use of liquid manure and nitrogenous fertilizers on fields.

The pollution of drinking water with pharmaceuticals has consequences: In Germany, scientists can observe that the fish population is becoming feminized, especially in the vicinity of sewage treatment plants.

The cause is believed to be hormones from contraception pills, which enter the water unfiltered through sewage treatment plants. So far, the government has not decreed a limit for hormones in tap water in the Drinking Water Ordinance. There is no regular monitoring of water bodies and drinking water for hormone residues. However, tests show that hormones and pharmaceuticals are regularly detected in our waters. In 2011, the Federal Environment Agency detected 23 active substances in drinking water and 55 in groundwater.

Random samples of drinking water in 69 German cities found residues of gadolinium, which is used as a contrast agent in magnetic resonance imaging (MRI). But it is not only this metal that is found in German drinking water. At times, the water is also polluted by pesticides and antibiotics. Therefore, it cannot be ruled out that these micro-pollutants may also pose a problem for drinking water and thus for humans in the long term.

The quality of tap water is guaranteed by the authorities only up to the house connection. With an average price per gallon of less than 0.87 cents, tap water is by far the cheapest drinking water.

TAP WATER - THE BEST TESTED FOOD?

Flavored Water

Mineral waters to which natural flavorings, fruit juice components or extracts are added are called " flavored water". In terms of food law, these products belong to the category of lemonades, as natural mineral water may not contain any additives other than carbon dioxide. However, you can also add ginger, mint leaves, limes, lime, etc. to the drinking water naturally to add flavor. Nowadays, the market also offers natural flavors to change the taste of our drinking water. Here it should be noted that these should not contain dyes or preservatives, are sugar-free and low in calories. Make sure to use only natural flavors instead of synthetic ones.

FLAVORED WATER - WATER WITH TASTE

Spring water

Similar to mineral water, spring water originates from underground water sources. Unlike mineral water, however, no official approval is required for spring water. There are no requirements for the demonstrability of positive effects on health and the content of contained minerals in spring water is allowed to fluctuate. However, one can be certain that spring water at least meets the quality requirements that are placed on tap water. It is subject to the same hygienic requirements as natural mineral water. However, in terms of chemical composition, it must correspond to drinking water. As with natural mineral water, treatment is not permitted.

SPRING WATER - HIGH QUALITY WATER

Healing Water

Healing waters are subject to the highest expectations. In addition to the requirements for natural mineral water, in Germany it is subject to the Medicines Act. It is approved by the Federal Institute for Drugs and Medical Devices. Only natural water that has been proven to have therapeutic benefits may be called healing water. Due to the composition of minerals, healing water can have a positive effect on health and especially prevent deficiency symptoms. Different types of healing water vary in their effects and possible areas of application. Healing water can be drunk daily without hesitation. It must be bottled exclusively at the source.

HEALING WATER - WATER WITH THERAPEUTIC BENEFITS

Holy springs

There are springs all over the world, most of which are religiously revered. Four of these springs are in Fatima (Portugal), Santiago de Compostela (Spain), Lourdes (France) and Medjugorje (Bosnia). The waters are said to have supernatural powers, they are said to make paralyzed people walk again, blind people see again, etc. Ever year, tens of thousands of people make pilgrimages to these places and ask for healing from their ailments. Years ago I also had an amazing experience with Lourdes water. A friend had offered me the water and claimed to have bottled it 30 years ago. It tasted fresh and energetic as if it came straight from the spring. In addition, the water showed no microbial contamination despite the long storage.

HOLY WELLS - SPECIAL WATER?

> *„If a government banned the drinking of water, it would become more popular than whiskey."*
>
> — Oscar Wilde

LIVING WATER
HEALTHY WATER

How does water get healthy information?

Water has several amazing attributes. The most fascinating one probably its ability to absorb and store information from the outside. With the term information, one can very easily see the connection to "computer science". The most important basis in computer science is two elements - the 1 and the 0. All the information I receive on the computer is actually a string of ones and zeros. Here, 1 stands for "true", 0 for "false", which can be transmitted, for example, by electrical voltage. A complex information can thus be presented only by means of these two basic elements.

An example:

01001100011010010110010101100010011001010

stands for the word "love".

Water also consists of two elements, so the molecule hydrogen and the molecule oxygen. These two form irregular molecular bundles (clusters). Clusters (string of molecules) are formed by information from outside and pass this information on (like in a computer) and this information is absorbed by the body and cells by drinking the water. The arrangement of the molecules as a cluster can be influenced from the outside. They assemble in accordance with an external source of information and result in their own information or identity, e.g. "sick" or "healthy". Information can flow into the water visually, acoustically or via frequencies. Thus, water can be addressed with texts, sonicated with melodies, influenced with images, informed with electromagnetic sound waves. Once the water has fully absorbed the information, it carries the imprint within itself and passes it on to its environment, including every cell of the body.

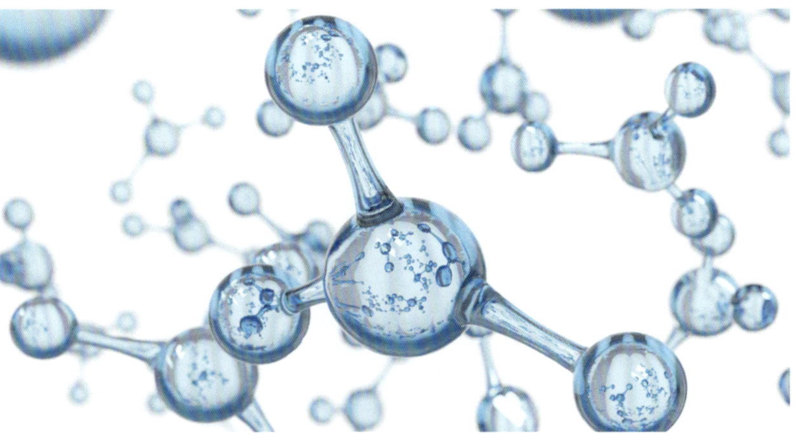

We drink this informed water (by the way, every water holds information, the question is whether it is positive or negative), which penetrates into our body and into all body cells and passes on its imprint. As a result, water influences our immunity and health like no other element. In addition, most of our body is precisely this instructed water.

In this way, the arrangement of water-oxygen molecule clusters in the figure below could have the imprint "health".

In nature, water is informed with a significant electro-magnetic frequency of stones or other sources of information. An example: Mineral waters are bottled at their sources, but then often transported over thousands of miles. Meanwhile, cell phone towers along the highways and toll bridges emit frequencies to their immediate surroundings. It is conceivable that these signals will also reach the mineral water bottles on the trucks.

What are frequencies?

Frequencies, vibration and radio waves are invisible. That is why we find it difficult to believe that they have an impact on physical objects. Only when we pick up our cell phone and make a call, no matter where, do we speak to our desired contact within seconds, all around the globe. When we turn on the TV and millions of points of light on the monitor create a moving picture in a fraction of a second, these are frequencies being transmitted into our home via satellite. Even if we ignore the effect of invisible frequencies like UV rays - as soon as we lie unprotected in the sun for a longer time, we can no longer doubt them.

FREQUENCIES CANNOT BE SEEN - BUT THEY DO WORK.

How do we now know that stones emit electromagnetic frequency?

About 20 years ago, the Swiss watch industry collapsed because a watch from the Seiko Company was launched in Japan, which revolutionized the entire watchmaking industry. A watch, which showed the time to the second for weeks, months, even years. Previously, no mechanical watch had been able to do this!

The secret was a small quartz crystal: it had such a precise oscillation that the clock deviated from its timekeeping accuracy by less than one second per day. As a result, the clock showed the time extremely accurate over a very long period of time. At last, after this technical marvel, frequency waves of stones are a part of publix awareness and do not have to be over and over again separately scientifically.

Of course, many scientists have researched and documented the effects of stones for thousands of years, most notably the abbess Hildegard of Bingen. The significant effect of stones was passed down from generation to generation. In literature we can find thousands of documentations dealing only with the effect of stones. I would especially like to emphasize my late friend Michael Gienger, who empirically researched stones for decades and published more than 30 best-selling books. For example, over several years, at various intervals, he sent out gemstones and minerals to more than 500 volunteers. They were given a questionnaire, which they returned to Michael Gienger. From these series of tests, he was able to summarize the significant properties of gemstones.

MAKE A CHOICE TO DRINK THE BEST WATER: CRYSTAL WATER

This example proves that vibrations of stones can give natural healthy information to the water and transform the molecular clusters to provide energy and health.

> *„When you drink water, consider its source."*
> — Chinese proverb

WHEN IS WATER HEALTHY AND SAFE?

Water has a healing or pathogenic effect on us humans, depending on its nature. Crucial to this are characteristics of the water that have been researched over a long period of time.

Dr. Louis Claude Vincent (University of Paris) received a research assignment from the French government to find out what properties water must possess in order to have a healthy and beneficial effect. From 1950 to 1974, 24 long years, Professor Vincent toured throughout France taking drinking water samples both in very small towns and in the big cities. As part of his research, Vincent conducted numerous studies on the properties of drinking water and their effects on human health. He compared the analyses with the statistics of health authorities and included countless values and parameters in his research. Along the Côte d'Azur, for example, he found extremely chalky, i.e. mineral-rich, water in addition to an extraordinarily high mortality rate of 13.4 per thousand - while Grenoble provided its inhabitants with very pure, soft drinking water. The mortality rate there was only 8.5 per thousand. In Marsat near Clermont-Ferrand, for example, the tap water was not chlorinated - cancer and cardiovascular diseases were hardly found there.

After years of studying various properties of drinking water (including many mineral waters), Prof. Vincent was finally able to define exactly how water impacts our health. He practically wrote a textbook on the nature of healthy water.

The analyses of his long-term studies showed that the r-value or electrical resistance of water and the pH value are the most important parameters for determining the quality of drinking water.

pH value

The pH value represents the proton concentration of a liquid and provides information on whether an aqueous solution is acidic or basic. According to Professor Vincent, the ideal pH value of drinking water is in the slightly acidic range between 6.4 and 6.8.

THE IDEAL PH-VALUE FOR DRINKING WATER IS BETWEEN 6.4 AND 6.8

Electrical resistance (R-value)

Electrical resistance, measured in ohms (Ω), is an accurate indicator of the purity of water. This is because pure water has the highest electrical resistance; the electrical conductivity, i.e. the reciprocal value, is almost zero for water. The proof is provided by distilled water (perfectly pure), which is used as an insulator between the electrically charged elements in car batteries.

PURE WATER IS THE BEST INSULATOR OF ELECTRICITY.

Nothing prevents the flow of electricity better than pure water. This refers to the purity of all substances dissolved in the water. The less dissolved solids (carbonates, sulfates, chlorides, etc.) the water contains, the higher its electrical resistance, i.e. the lower its electrical conductivity. This is because it is the mineral salts and toxins dissolved in the water that perform the function of a conductor of electricity. Electrical conductivity is measured in microsegments (μS).

According to Professor Vincent, water with a high electrical resistance, corresponding to a low electrical conductivity, is more easily absorbed by the organism. This means that the lower the electrical conductivity and the less lime, salts and other conductive substances, including toxins, are dissolved in the water, the healthier it is. There are measuring devices (approx. 25 EUR) that show the exact electrical conductivity of water within seconds. In this way, you can check your own water purity and the content of current-conducting substances very precisely and quickly. According to Professor Vincent, the optimal resistance value is below 130 µS.

Here is a classification of water quality according to electrical conductivity in µS:

0–89 µS	Very good purifying/detoxifying effect
90–129 µS	Good purifying/detoxifying effect
130–199 µS	Still satisfying purifying/detoxifying effect
200–299 µS	No more effect - first deposits in the blood vessels
300–499 µS	Already straining - contamination of blood vessels
500–1299 µS	Bad for health - high contamination of blood vessels
1300–2500 µS	Highly stressful - very high contamination of the blood vessels

As an example, tap water with a hardness level of 14 corresponds to an electrical resistance of 2500 Ω or a conductance of 400 µS. The water is considered already polluting and without purifying effect, pollutants and acids remain in the body.

PURE WATER HAS THE BEST PURIFYING AND DETOXIFYING EFFECT ON THE ORGANISM. WATER IS LIFE.

Fundamentally, Dr. Vincent provided evidence that cardiovascular disease and cancer are significantly more common in regions with high-salt, high-calcium, hard drinking water than in areas with soft drinking water with reduced salt or lime levels.

HEALTHY WATER IS HEALTHY LIFE.

> *„We drink 90 percent of our diseases.“*
> — Louis Pasteur, French microbiologist

METHODS
TO IMPROVE YOUR DRINKING WATER'S QUALITY AT HOME

For anyone who wants to further improve the supply of drinking water from the tap itself, there are various methods of consumer water treatment:

Distillation:

A still produces soft, clean drinking water obtained by the steam distillation process. Water is brought to the boiling point, and the rising water vapor condenses in a cooling coil. Subsequently, the water is freed from any pollutants and residues such as heavy metals, drug residues and lime by an activated carbon filter. One distillation cycle takes about four hours. A distillation process guarantees harmless, crystal-clear, soft drinking water at all times with consistent, maximum purity. The device offers several advantages:

- Removes all pollutants from tap water
- Removes residues such as lime and rust
- No loss of performance due to clogged filters
- Unattended operation possible (for example at night)
- No installation, no connection
- No drilling necessary low operating costs

DISTILLATION PRODUCES THE PUREST WATER.

Disinfection with ozone

An ozone system can be easily integrated into an existing water treatment system or into the main pipeline. Ozone is more successful at inactivating viruses and bacteria than any other disinfection treatment while requiring very little contact time, shortening treatment time and eliminating the need for chemical agents.

Due to its high oxidation potential, ozone effectively breaks down microbes and viruses. Ozone can be used to oxidize hydrocarbons in cellular lipid bilayers, which kills contaminating microbes.

Ozone treatment also prevents regrowth of microorganisms. Ozonation provides protection against virtually all undesirable microbes. After treatment, the ozone in the water is naturally broken down.

OZONE EFFECTIVELY BREAKS DOWN MICROBES AND VIRUSES AND PREVENTS THE REGROWTH OF HARMFUL MICROORGANISMS.

Reverse osmosis

This water filtration system can be either mounted under the sink or positioned as an attractive eye-catcher. The systems use the principle of reverse osmosis for water treatment.

This natural way of water treatment gives the purest water. The principle of reverse osmosis was developed by NASA back in the 1960s to make astronauts' urine drinkable again.

Contaminated water, so-called concentrate, is forced through a membrane. The water that has passed through the small holes is called permeate and is free of any contaminants. The membrane has microscopic holes that are produced with a laser.

The diameter of the holes is just large enough for a water molecule to fit through. Since the water molecule has the smallest diameter, all other molecules, including pollutant molecules, remain in the membrane.

For water purity, reverse osmosis water is comparable to distilled water. After the water is pushed past the membrane, the contaminated water flows back into the wastewater.

Meanwhile, the ratio of pure water to wastewater at these plants is close to 2:1. This means to produce 34 fl.oz. of pure water, it takes 68 fl.oz. of tap water.

**REVERSE OSMOSIS FILTERS ALL MOLECULES
LARGER THAN WATER MOLECULES
FROM TAP WATER.**

Activated carbon filtration by means of carbon filter

Characteristic of this process of water filtration is that the water passes through a granulated layer of carbon particles. Optionally, the water can be filtered through several layers. Because the activated carbon is treated with oxygen, millions of small pores form between the carbon (carbon) atoms. Due to the size of the surface of activated carbon, countless binding spots are thus formed. With this principle, the water is cleaned from chemicals and impurities. When the contaminants in the water reach the carbon particles, they are contained there and cannot continue to flow with the water. An activated carbon filter is a chemical absorption process. These systems are inexpensive because, apart from water pressure, they do not require any energy source. As long as the consumer maintains control of optimal functionality by regularly changing filters and maintaining water pressure, these filter systems are effective for water treatment.

- Activated carbon filters work without electricity and do not waste water.

- They not only improve the taste and smell of the filtered water, but also remove all coarse and fine pollutants such as chlorine and other impurities from the water.

- Due to the loose arrangement of the granulated carbon material, the water flow is not obstructed. Therefore, a carbon filter can be used in any home water treatment system.

- This filtration system leaves essential trace minerals and other healthy minerals such as magnesium, calcium or potassium in the water.

- The removal of concentrated chemicals such as chlorine, trihalomethanes, fluoride, coarse contaminants with e.g. organic material such as humus or algae and microscopic contaminants such as Herbicides and pesticides is no problem with this.

You should know, however, that the carbon will only react chemically with the pollutants as long as the carbon molecules are not saturated. Once the carbon filter is saturated, the water flows past the carbon particles unfiltered and all the pollutants re-enter the drinking water. Therefore, it is important to change the carbon filters regularly. Unfortunately, the manufacturer's specifications for the shelf life of the carbon filters are very optimistic. I recommend changing the carbon filters much earlier than recommended by the manufacturer. It is more costly, but safer.

ACTIVATED CARBON BONDS ALL POLLUTANTS.

Levitate water:

The water researcher Wilfried Hacheney (1924-2010) developed the process of being able to "levitate" water. By that, he didn't mean he could make it float.

He wanted "levitation" to be understood as the opposite of gravitation, since the water is pulled apart by the forces acting on it during the process and would not be pressed together by gravity as under normal circumstances. However, there are no studies that prove the effect of his procedure. Levitated water is vortexed and is said to be healthier than regular tap water. To understand the special property of levitated water, you have to know a chemical property of the water molecules: They each have one oxygen atom and two hydrogen atoms. The two hydrogen atoms of a water molecule each have an attraction to the oxygen atom of another, neighboring water molecule. Due to this attraction, the molecules bond with each other. Proponents of levitated water believe that water molecules form solid compounds called clusters even in the liquid state. This is especially enhanced when water is forced through pipes at high pressure, up to 40 bar. The problem is that the clusters can pass on negative information. Through levitation, according to Hacheneye's method, it should be possible to disrupt the clusters in tap water. This makes levitated water healthy - if you believe the supporters of this theory.

LEVITATING IS SUPPOSED TO DISSOLVE UNHEALTHY CLUSTER INFORMATION IN WATER.

Crystal water

Whether it is devastating droughts or horrific floods, nature is the most powerful force on our planet and has a comprehensive impact on our lives. It constantly shows us the impressive effects of its power - like in the regeneration and vitalization of water. Water falls as rain on the earth, seeps into the ground, runs against or over stones and flows out at the source as magnificent water. It follows an important principle:

"Element Stone Regenerates Element Water." No water is healthier and more energetic than spring water.

But how does this phenomenon of revitalization work? We know that every stone emits vibrations to the environment. This sounds metaphysical, but since the invention of the quartz watch, we know that stones or quartz crystals produce oscillations. The realization of the oscillation frequency of quartz was a tremendous revolution for the watch industry. Of course, we also know from crystal healing through numerous studies that stones have had an effect on their environment for thousands of years. The quartz clock also brought scientific certainty about this. VitaJuwel products take advantage of this natural principle: "Element stone regenerates element water"! Now some may ask how the vibrations work through the glass. The answer is very simple: any vibration or frequency, be it radio waves or UV rays, penetrates barriers, especially since glass is molten stone.

Studies have shown that these frequencies take about seven minutes to completely restructure the water in a natural way. Now, no ordinary stones are used, but precious stones. Therefore, it is reasonable to assume that you drink not only regenerated, but the best regenerated water in the world.

In 2008, VitaJuwel won the much sought-after "Gastronomic Innovation of the Year" award. As a prize, VitaJuwel was reimbursed for a costly laboratory test that checked the contamination of water on a daily basis. In this laboratory test, no germs developed in the gem water within 12 months - it was as fresh and uncontaminated as it was on the first day. This is proof of the quality of this water treatment!

CRYSTAL WATER IS THE MOST NATURAL WAY TO TREAT WATER.

> *„Everything has sprung from the water!*
> *Everything is preserved by water!"*
>
> — Johann Wolfgang von Goethe

INSTITUE FOR
WATER ANALYSIS

There are some German institutes that test the quality of tap water on request. This way, you can be sure to drink tap water with a clear conscience:

https://www.wasserschnelltest.de
This institute offers over a dozen different water analyses, ranging from an analysis for lead in the water for 25 Euros to a high-quality analysis for pesticides or plant protection agents in the drinking water, which detects over 460 different active substances.

https://www.igb.fraunhofer.de
The Fraunhofer Institute for Interfacial Engineering and Biotechnology IGB develops and optimizes processes and products for the business areas of health, chemicals and process industry, and environment and energy. They analyze drinking water using state-of-the-art methods and provide a comprehensive, reliable and quality-assured assessment of water.

https://www.institut-fresenius.de/de
SGS INSTITUT FRESENIUS tests, analyzes and evaluates water for significant components.

https://www.eurofins.de/umwelt
Eurofins Institut Jäger GmbH is a specialized environmental laboratory with headquarters in Tübingen. The main focus of work is on the analysis and evaluation of drinking water, mineral water, groundwater and wastewater.

https://www.wassertest-online.de
In this institute, water can be tested for pollutants. It offers a water analysis kit for consumers to collect and test water. Simple sampling incl. instructions, no previous knowledge necessary, water analysis in accredited water laboratory according to DIN-EN-ISO 17025.

INFLUENTAL WATER RESEARCHERS

Water is our most important nutrient, so it is consistent that capacities all over the world have been and are dealing with the phenomenon of "water". I would like to introduce some researchers who have discovered new secrets from water.

Masaru Emoto

Masaru Emoto was the first to photograph the crystals of frozen water. Under the most difficult conditions, breathtaking images of water from all over the world were created - fascinating impressions that open our senses and hearts to the profound external influences on our water (See In his bestseller "The Hidden Messages in Water") he explains new revolutionary theses about the secrets of water. I had been friends with him, many of our insights on water were in common.

Viktor Schauberger

The Austrian forester and inventor Viktor Schauberger (1885-1958) had the rare gift of being able to see nature in the cards. However, it requires a talent that can hardly be underestimated to look into his own cards, since his written legacy is often difficult to understand. Today he is considered a pioneer of modern water research and holistic observation of nature. His discovery was the self-purification and vitalization of water through turbulence by means of special funnels or spiral pipes. Schauberger formulated his "k&k principle" as early as the first half of the 20th century: one must first understand nature and then copy it.

Fereydoon Batmanghelidj

"You're not sick - you're thirsty!" This is the powerful message of the Iranian physician F. Batmanghelidj, who shakes up the paradigm of Western medicine and places water itself at the center of self-healing. He healed tens of thousands of people in his lifetime using only water. Numerous books document his unique research on the healing power of water. As a political prisoner, he spent some time in prison, and there, due to a lack of medication, he discovered the healing power of water.

Prof. Gerald H. Pollack

He is recognized as the most important water scientist of modern times and revolutionized water knowledge with the realization that water can not only have the three known aggregate states liquid, solid and gaseous, but that there is a fourth aggregate state. In this process, the water reaches an absolutely pure state with a negative electrical charge. He is the leading expert in the field of water structure research. He has received numerous awards and various honors for his extensive research. As a professor of bioengineering at the University of Washington, he is in charge of the "Pollack Laboratory". The fascination of water and its secrets have been researched by many luminaries in our several thousand years of history, and some insights have been gained. However, the phenomenon of water still remains a mystery in many areas.

> *„Knowledge and science are not the same thing.*
> *Knowledge is the whole, science is a part.*
>
> — Count Leo Nikolajewitsch Tolstoi

MASARU EMOTO

Masaru Emoto was a Japanese scientist and alternative physician, he is one of the great famous water scientists in the world. He has been working with water since the early 1990s. According to his research, water can absorb and store the influences of thoughts, feelings, sounds and frequencies. He achieved these insights by experiments with bottled water, which he labeled with either positive messages such as "thank you" or negative messages such as "war" and then froze it at minus 30 degrees Celsius and photographed it with an electron microscope as it thawed. In this way, he established a visually recognizable connection between the appearance of the ice crystal and the quality or condition of the water. Emoto's findings revolutionized the way water is perceived. He expressed his insights in the worldwide bestseller "The Hidden Messages in Water." This book was number one on the New York Times bestseller list for years

In early 2009, his office in Japan asked if he could visit us. We agreed and just one week later he visited our company. We had a very interesting day together and could validate each other in all the experiences gained. Three key insights emerged from our joint conversation:

1. Water voraciously absorbs information of all kinds and reshapes its own molecular structure according to these new instructions and passes them on to the environment.

2. Water cannot be studied in a double-blind study because the water in the jars in the laboratory is constantly exposed to new influences and it is constantly changing. When the employees in the laboratory talk to each other, this new information is immediately transferred to the water and the water reshapes itself.

3. Decisive for the effect of drinking water on the body is not only the biological quality of the water, but to the same extent the consciousness with which the person drinks the water.

Emoto's many photographs are sensational, where he photographed frozen water drops, which he instructed individually beforehand. He labeled the water container or the water with terms, talked to it with words or phrases, or he sounded it with music. Here are some of his epoch-making water photographs:

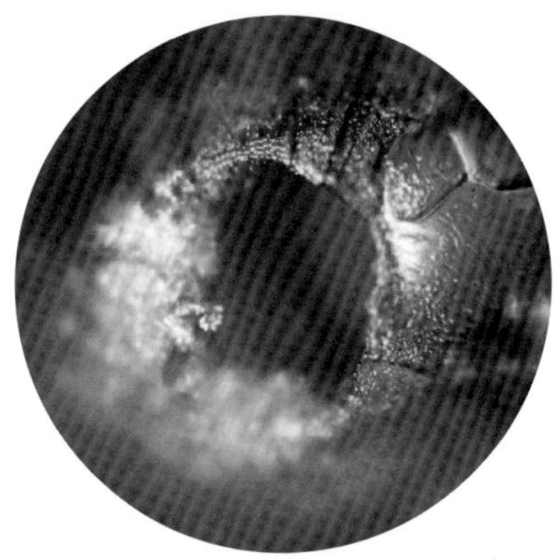

tap water
from Scheidegg, Germany

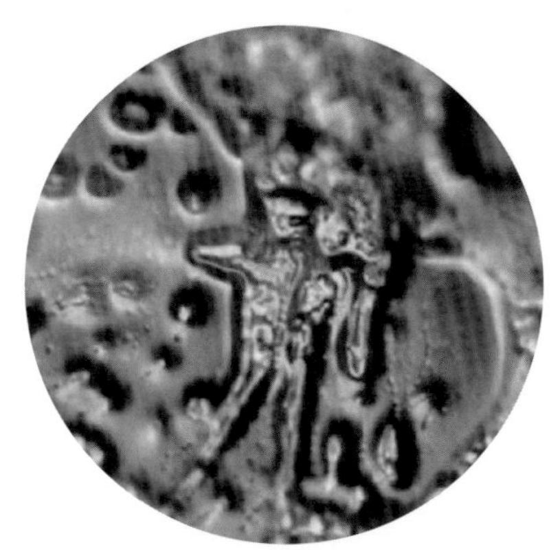

water with
„You make me sick"
spoken to it

tap water with
„Health"
spoken to it

water with
Mozart's symphonies
played to it

water with
„diamond"
spoken to it

water with
„Love and Peace"
spoken to it

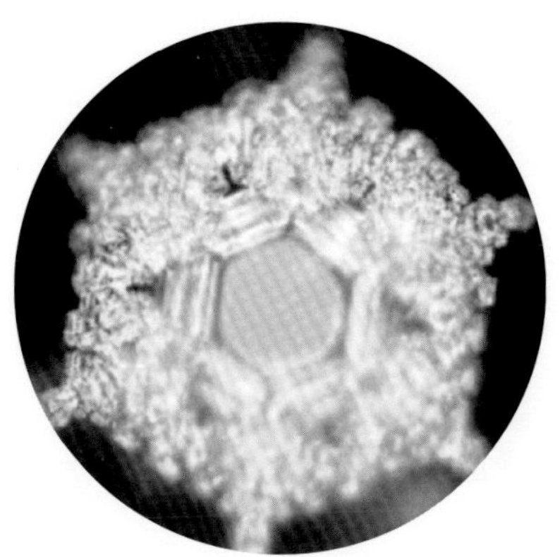

water with
„Love and Gratitude"
spoken to it

But what made an extremely lasting impression on me was that when he visited me, he asked me to give him a piece of paper with my signature on it. Weeks later I got an email from him where he opened up that he had stuck the piece of paper with my signature on a glass of water for 24 hours and then frozen a drop of water from that glass. He then photographed the water drop as it thawed. He attached the picture of my own water crystal. Subsequently, he analyzed my water crystal and was able to explain things about me that only my immediate family, and in some cases only I, had knowledge of. Scars on my body, experiences from my birth and my past and more were read from my ice crystal image.

> *„The heart is a crystal temple.“*
>
> — Japanese proverb

DR. FEREYDOON BATMANGHELIDJ

Dr. Batmanghelidj completed his medical training at St Mary's Hospital, London University. He returned to Iran and was arrested there by the Iranian revolutionary government. By his own admission, he discovered the "healing power of water" in prison. Because there was no medical care in the prisons at the time and no medication was available, Dr. Fereydoon Batmanghelidj treated his fellow prisoners only with water - with considerable success.

According to Batmanghelidj, dehydration has far more impact on health than commonly thought, and to be the cause of many diseases (e.g., cancer, strokes, depression coronary heart disease, osteoporosis, gout, or obesity). In 1982 Batmanghelidj emigrated from Iran to the USA. Here he lectured and wrote several books on the subject. His number one message was, "You're not sick, you're thirsty!"

The intention of Dr. Fereydoon Batmanghelidj is to educate on the importance of water for wellness based on the latest findings in microanatomy and molecular physiology. For him, chronic water shortage is the main cause of many diseases. Some say this realization is the greatest achievement of modern medicine. Understanding the importance of chronic water deficiency laid the foundation for the development of a more humane health system.

CHRONIC WATER DEFICIENCY IS THE MAIN CAUSE OF MANY DISEASES.

He believes people can be decisively healthier and more productive in the future at a cost that is 70% less than today's healthcare costs. History teaches us that we often make important leaps in development when we recognize the basic techniques that nature uses. Nature has provided that the human body consists of more than 70 percent water. If the natural balance is present, there is a high probability that the person will be healthy and active; if there is an imbalance, e.g. dehydration (lack of water), complications occur that can manifest itself as disease. In the case of prolonged water deficiency, chronic conditions may even develop.

Here are reports by Dr. Batmanghelidj, from his book "You are not sick - you are thirsty", on the subject of water deficiency in the body and on healing successes with water drinking:

„Twenty years ago I began to treat stomach ulcers with water. Over the course of two years and seven months, I successfully treated more than 3000 cases. From this experience I learned that the people in question were in fact thirsty, and that we physicians had labeled an expression of thirst in the human organism as a disease. I also came to this conclusion because a number of other diseases also responded to increased water intake. The treatments were done with nothing but plain tap water. I discovered the phenomenon that "pain" in the organism is often simply a sign of thirst.I set out to provide scientific proof of my discovery that pain is a sign of a lack of water in the organism. I first spent four years reading scientific articles, sometimes up to eighteen hours a day, as well as congress reports on neurotransmitters or books on biophysics to understand the relationship between water and life. I was convinced that the answers could only be found in these publications, not in the medical journals. And I was to be proven right.

I discovered a serious flaw in the medical understanding of the human organism: it is not the solids that regulate all the functions of the organism; rather, it is the water that dissolves all the solids circulating in the blood and provides the energy for the chemical reactions of all the functions of the organism. In a nutshell, water is the essential regulator. Everything else is subordinate to it.

Feeling of thirst: The feeling of thirst is an unreliable indicator of the state of chronic water deficiency in the cells of the human organism. Chronic pain can be considered as indicators of an improper water balance.

In any case, water deficiency does not manifest itself in a single symptom, but rather in a series of concurrent problems that resolve themselves when sufficient water is available.

Not only does it appear that my research has brought to light the primary cause of pain and degenerative disease, but it has also become clear in what uncomplicated ways the latter can be prevented: Prevent the lack of water to prevent disease!"

WATER CAN CURE DISEASES, CONSOLIDATE HEALTH AND PROLONG ACTIVE LIFE.

The German Nutrition Society (Deutsche Gesellschaft für Ernährung e. V.) recommends drinking a healthy amount of water of 1 to 1.4 flo.z. per kilogram (= 2.2 lbs) of body weight. For a woman weighing 121 lbs., this means drinking 68 fl.oz., and for a man weighing 155 lbs., 101.5 fl.oz. of healthy water.

Thus, we no longer have to rely on our unreliable sense of thirst but revitalize our bodies with continuous drinking spread throughout the day. This ensures optimal care of all organs and prevention of diseases and premature aging.

Therefore, a good supply of healthy water for the body is the best health care that each individual can provide for himself without much effort and expense. In another chapter, I give 14 tips to ensure optimal water intake, spread over the day.

> *„Water tastes good - does good - is good!"*

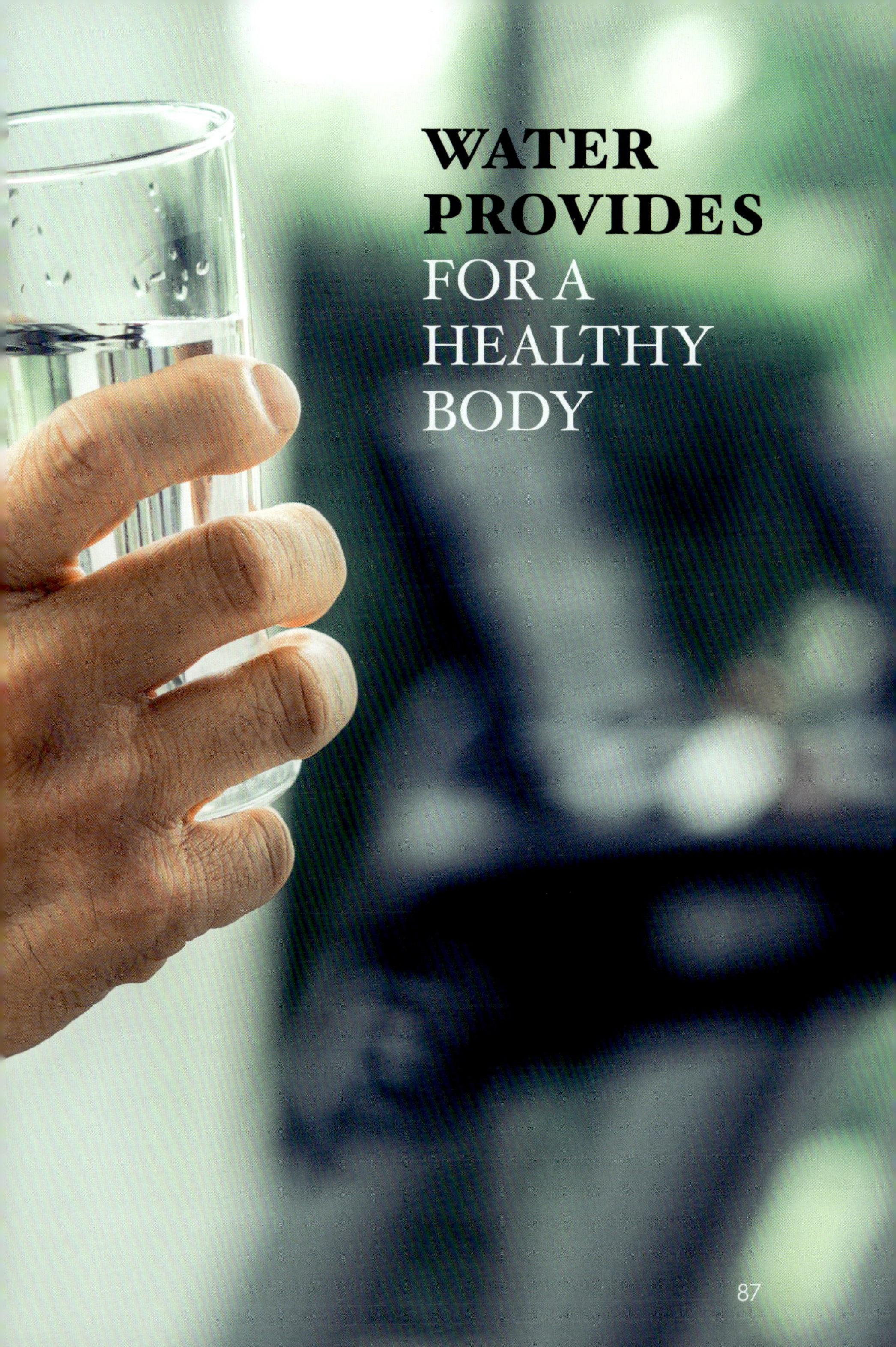

WATER PROVIDES FOR A HEALTHY BODY

Water guarantees optimal health and a long, active life. Drinking plenty of water can help alleviate or prevent certain illnesses.

However, if more water is lost through the kidneys, lungs, skin, respiration and bowel movements (feces) than is supplied to the body, the result is a lack of water in the body (dehydration). We already get a feeling of thirst when our total body water is reduced by 0.5 percent. The more the body's water level decreases, the stronger not only our thirst becomes, but also the more the fluidity of our blood is affected. Urea-containing substances are then also no longer excreted in sufficient quantities. If we lose 3 percent of our body water, our mental and physical performance declines, and our ability to concentrate and react are particularly affected. If we lose 5 percent of our total body water and do not compensate for this in time, this can lead to an accelerated pulse, increased body temperature and circulatory weakness. At a loss of 10 percent, confusion may also occur. Finally, a loss of more than 20 percent of body fluid leads to a life-threatening condition due to circulatory and kidney failure.

JUST A LOSS OF THREE PERCENT OF BODY WATER LIMITS BODILY AND MENTAL PERFORMANCE CONSIDERABLY.

Healthy water accordingly also has a direct positive influence on physical impairments. Here are three examples:

Constipation: Constipation is not a disease, but a symptom - a sign that something is wrong in the body. It can severely affect the quality of life of those affected: Emptying the bowels is difficult and painful.

In addition to sufficient exercise, a diet rich in fiber, and rest when eating, healthy water in sufficient quantities, e.g. a glass of water in the morning on an empty stomach, is an effective means of alleviating or preventing constipation.

Urinary tract infection: Women in particular often suffer from bladder infections, but older men are also frequently affected. Bladder infections are usually noticeable by burning pain during urination. Urinary tract infections are triggered by bacteria that usually come from the intestines. They cause inflammation in the urethra and bladder. Depending on the type of germs, healthy water can make life difficult for the bacteria and flush out the germs. My recommendation: in case of chronic urinary tract infections drink up to 84.5 fl.oz. of high-energy water every day. It is best to spread this amount evenly throughout the day and drink the last portion directly before going to bed. Those who wake up at night can drink another glass.

Decreasing eyesight: Drinking more than 84.5 fl.oz. of healthy water a day will improve your eyesight. This measurably increases near and distance vision by up to 0.5 diopters. Plenty of fluid improves the flow of blood and thus the blood supply to the retina and the optic nerve tissue. However, this effect does not occur with sugary thirst quenchers, since sugared drinks bind the water and thicken the blood.

Water also helps you absorb important vitamins, minerals and nutrients from your food and eliminate harmful toxins from your body, increasing your chances of staying healthy.

WATER A BLESSING FOR OUR BODY

Nothing affects our body and our health more than water. 70 percent water content in our bodies ensures well-being, higher immunity, better health and a longer, more active life. Because those who do not get sick live longer and are more active.

This list indicates how much water is contained in specific organs. It shows how important water is for their function:

- Vitreous body of the eye = 99 percent percent
- Blood plasma = 90 percent
- Brain (gray matter) = 84 percent
- Lungs = 84 percent
- Blood = 80 percent
- Kidney = 79 percent
- Heart = 74 percent
- Skin = 72 percent
- Spinal cord = 71 percent
- Brain (white matter) = 70 percent
- Bone = 50 percent
- Fat tissue = 25 percent
- Hair = 4 percent

> *„Whoever understands the effects of water and knows how to use it in ist exceedingly manifold ways possesses a remedy which cannot be surpassed by any other. None is more varied in ist effect."*
>
> — Pastor Sebastian Kneipp —

Water makes up a large part of the body's weight and is part of many important functions:

1. **It helps to produce saliva**
Water is a major component of saliva. Saliva also contains small amounts of electrolytes, mucus and enzymes. It is a solvent for food nutrients, which can only be detected in dissolved form by the taste receptors in the tongue.

Saliva contains mucins, the "lubricants" of the oral cavity. They facilitate the chewing and swallowing of solid food ingredients. In addition, the mucus film they form on the oral cavity wall protects the underlying cell layer from injury and dehydration. It contains digestive enzymes such as the fat-splitting lipase and the carbohydrate-splitting -amylase. Other enzymes included are lysozyme and peroxidase. Lysozyme can break down wall components of bacteria; peroxidase has non-specific antibacterial and antiviral properties. Saliva also contains immunoglobulin A: this type of antibody can fend off pathogens.

Saliva moistens the oral cavity, which is important for clear pronunciation. It keeps the mouth clean by continuously rinsing the oral cavity and teeth.

2. **It regulates your body temperature**
Why is a balanced body temperature between 36 and 37 degrees Celsius essential for our health?

The formation of enzymes and hormones, in fact the entire metabolic activity, only occurs optimally in a certain temperature range.

Without the effective cooling system of our sweat glands, life would not be possible. The human being is an equal-warmed living being. That means it regulates its body temperature via a form of cooling produced by the evaporation of water. When sweat evaporates on the skin, energy is consumed in the form of heat.

This heat in turn is extracted from the body, so it is cooled. This makes us relatively independent of the ambient temperature and allows us to keep our body temperature constant.

When the organism heats up in the blazing sun, during strenuous physical activity or in the sauna, the surplus body heat is released through sweating. Most people also start to sweat when they get excited or eat spicy foods.

As soon as a critical situation occurs, the nerve cells send an alarm signal to the brain. This instantly activates approximately two to four million sweat glands, which begin producing sweat. Sweat also keeps the skin's protective acid mantle in balance by inhibiting the growth of germs on the skin's surface. The glandular secretion contributes to a healthy and balanced skin flora with this natural barrier protective function. The number of microorganisms such as bacteria and fungi is "kept in check" by the slightly acidic pH of the sweat.

However, sweating causes the body to lose electrolytes and plasma. Therefore, adequate water intake is vital to prevent mineral loss and dehydration.

If water would not be used to regulate body temperature, i.e. to cool it, the same thing would happen just like the terrible disaster in Fukushima: we would overheat, collapse and ultimately die.

3. It protects the tissues, spinal cord and joints

Herniated discs have now become a widespread disease. Our 23 intervertebral discs serve as a buffer and suspension between the vertebrae. Thus, the intervertebral discs often bear many times our body weight.

The intervertebral disc is one of the bradytrophic tissue types with a lower blood flow and a slower metabolism. Supply is via diffusion, the flow of fluid triggered by movement and compression. In the process, the intervertebral disc absorbs water and nutrients from the surrounding tissue fluid like a sponge - especially at night. During the day, while active, some of the fluid is forced back out of the disc due to the weight of the body while standing and sitting. Increasingly more sitting activities at work and everyday life and insufficient water supply are mainly responsible for the specific wear and tear of the intervertebral discs. In the long term, undernourished "joint buffers" lose their ability to adequately cushion shocks.

4. Drinking water helps to lubricate joints and spinal cord and to keep them flexible.

Car and industrial complexes exhaust fumes, heavy metals, environmental toxins, bacteria, fungi, parasites, herbicides, pesticides, insecticides, plasticizers from packaging materials, preservatives and dyes, pharmaceuticals, mold toxins, acids - all the pollutants we take in through the air we breathe, the food we eat, the water we drink, and our skin become part of our metabolism and thus of our organism. Metabolism is the sum of all chemical processes in the body that convert substances from food, drinking water and breathing air to build up or maintain body tissue and generate energy for our daily lives.

Of course, these polluting substances damage our metabolism as "slags". If the stress gets out of hand, we are surprised when we catch colds, experience sudden immune deficiencies in the form of allergies, and simply feel unwell often due to minor aches and pains in our daily lives. In fact, only healthy water has sufficient solvent capacity to absorb the unwanted waste in the body and dispose of it through the excretory organs such as kidneys, bladder, liver and intestines. Water provides consistency to the stool in the intestines to prevent constipation. Our kidneys are important for flushing out body waste through urination. At the same time, with healthy water, the excretory and filtering organs receive enough energy to do an excellent job of the detoxification process.

Here is my recommendation to detoxify the body in the best possible way with a drinking cure: drink about 10 fl.oz. of lukewarm water in the morning directly after getting up (before breakfast). This has a very fine, quasi "crystalline" cluster structure. Such water can optimally perform the task as a transport medium for nutrients into the cell and waste products out of the cell.

5. It helps to improve physical performance

Drinking plenty of water during physical activity is essential. Athletes can lose 6 to 10 percent of their body weight during physical activity. Negative effects of exercise without enough water can include serious medical impairments such as decreased blood pressure and hyperthermia.

That's why you should drink sufficient amounts of water before and after every sporting activity - in the best case also more than the required 68 fl.oz. per day.

6. It supports healthy bowel movement

Healthy water before, during and after a meal will help the body digest food more easily. Water ensures effective digestion and utilization of food. It not only helps to break down food, but also dissolves vitamins, minerals and other nutrients from food. This ensures good care of the cells.

7. It helps lose weight

Some studies have linked body fat and weight loss in overweight girls and women to drinking more water. Drinking more water while dieting and exercising can help you lose extra pounds. Water fills the stomach and dilutes the "hunger hormone" ghrelin, which is partly produced in the stomach lining - effectively reducing an increased feeling of hunger.

8. It improves blood circulation and supply of oxygen

Blood is the body fluid that, with the support of the cardiovascular system, ensures the functionality of the various body tissues through a variety of transport and interconnecting functions. Blood is referred to as "fluid tissue," and occasionally as a "fluid organ." Blood consists of special cells as well as the protein-rich blood plasma, which acts as a carrier for these cells in the cardiovascular system. It performs many essential tasks in the body with its individual components. Its main task is to transport oxygen and nutrients to the cells and to remove metabolic end products such as carbon dioxide or urea. It also transports hormones and other active components between the cells. 55 percent of the blood is blood plasma, which consists of up to 95 percent water, the rest being other substances dissolved in the carrier water. The ions present in plasma are predominantly sodium, chloride, potassium, magnesium, phosphate and calcium ions.

The quantity of proteins is about 60 to 80 g/l, corresponding to 8 percent of the plasma volume. Plasma proteins perform tasks of substance transport, immune defense, blood clotting, maintenance of pH and osmotic pressure.

As part of the immune system, blood has tasks such as protection and defense against foreign bodies and antigens by phagocytes (scavenger cells) and by antibodies. Further, blood is an important component in the response to injury (blood clotting and fibrinolysis). The body of a person weighing about 155 lbs. contains between 170 and 203 fl.oz. blood. Blood is our elixir of life and performs all life-sustaining, especially health-sustaining tasks in our body. Since blood consists of 95 percent water, it is self-explanatory that healthy water also forms healthy and energy-rich blood. A balanced daily water intake improves circulation and has a positive effect on overall health.

9. It is used to combat diseases

Healthy water not only strengthens our immunity and protects us from diseases, it also helps our body to successfully cure diseases. Pathogens are flushed out more quickly and metabolic processes run optimally when we drink enough water. Certain diseases react particularly positively to fluid intake:

- Constipation
- Exercise-induced asthma
- Urinary tract infection
- Hypertension

By drinking enough water, you increase your chances of absorbing important vitamins, minerals, and nutrients from your food to boost your overall constitution and stay healthy.

10. It helps to increase energy

One study found that drinking 16.9 fl.oz. of water increased metabolic rate by 30 percent in both men and women. These effects seemed to last for over an hour. When all body functions work optimally through sufficient intake of healthy water, it is logical that our performance and sense of well-being reach a much higher level.

11. Water is the main component in both the lymph and other body fluids

Lymph fulfills two functions in the body: On the one hand, it is part of the immune system by transporting pathogens to the lymph nodes, and on the other hand, it transports molecules that are too large to be transported directly from the tissues into the bloodstream, such as proteins and lipids from the digestive tract.

The lymph circulates in the lymphatic vessels. These collect the plasma that does not return directly from the tissues into the capillaries and return it centrally to the veins. Water, as with our blood, is the most important ingredient for healthy liquidity of our lymph.

Other body fluids that depend on adequate water intake include:

- Gastric fluid, also called stomach acid, is a more or less viscous and clear liquid of strongly acidic reaction. The reaction comes from the hydrochloric acid contained in the gastric fluid, which is an important component of gastric fluid.

- The secretion of the pancreas contains various digestive enzymes, which also serve to break down proteins. These enter the duodenum via excretory ducts that join the common bile duct. The secretion is a protein-rich alkaline fluid with a pH of 7 to 8. Approximately 50.7 fl.oz. are produced per day.

12. Water boosts brain activity

Our brain has a water content of over 90 percent. One can imagine that in the case of a water deficiency, the brain is affected first and foremost. Fatigue, lack of concentration, slower thinking, declining attention, etc. are the immediate symptoms.

A study involving over 180 subjects has produced sensational results. These people drank 68 fl.oz. of healthy water a day for two weeks and experienced amazing results:

- The speed at which information was processed in the brain increased by 6 percent.
- The attention span increased by 9 percent.
- The working memory of the brain showed an increase of 15 percent. Our working memory in the brain is the center for processing conscious information and an important basis for our intellectual performance.

Additional findings from the study:

- Impreved mental resilience and mental fitness
- Self-confidence and a deeper psychological balance
- Increased vitality, joie de vivre, new sense of well-being and drive for activity

A group of high school graduates was tested to see how grades were related to the amount they drank each day. Indicators of mental performance clearly proved that those who drank around 68 to 101.5 fl.oz. of water a day had better grades in their final exams.

13. Healthy water helps to improve the mood

Too little water can also affect your mood. Dehydration can cause fatigue and confusion as well as anxiety. As also shown by the additional findings of the study mentioned in point 12, water can brighten your mood, boost your self-confidence and increase your optimism.

14. Water rejuvenates the skin

The skin is the largest organ of the body. This makes it all the more important to supply the skin with sufficient healthy water. The skin has a variety of roles. As a stable but flexible shell, it protects the body from harmful environmental influences such as wetness, cold and sunlight, as well as from pathogens and toxins. The complexion of the skin provides a whole range of information at a glance - for example, about age and state of health. The skin also serves as a large storage area for the body: water and fat can be stored in the sub cutis, but also metabolic products. It also produces hormones that are important for the whole body.

A pilot study of the Charité came to the following conclusion: Drinking water promotes the vitality of his skin. 10 minutes after drinking, the skin is better supplied with blood and oxygen and thus the skin metabolism is "boosted". The increased metabolic activity supports the protective and defense function of the skin. This internal "Vitalization Effect" is noticeable in the long term in a healthier appearance of the skin.

> *„The body is an inscription, written on water.“*
>
> —— Indian Wisdom ——

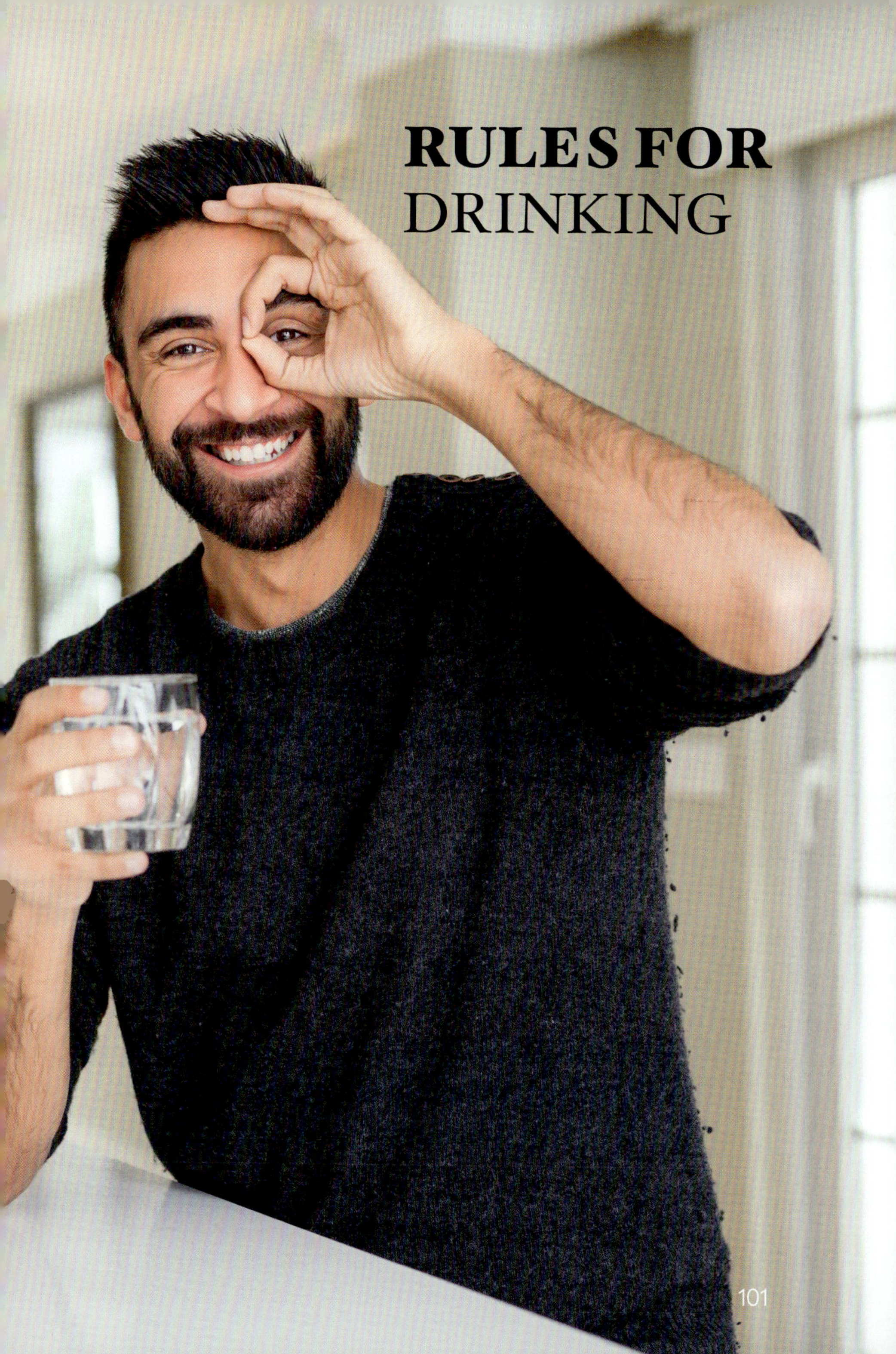
RULES FOR
DRINKING

Adequate hydration is extremely important for all vital bodily functions to work at their best, and yet we often forget to drink sufficient amounts in our daily lives. The following tips and tricks should help you drink adequate amounts of healthy water every day:

- Drinking water continuously throughout the day is something that works – even with lots of discipline – only for a short period of time.

- Always place a bottle or pitcher of healthy water within easy reach at your workstation, on your desk or at your machine.

- At home, for example when watching TV or reading, a drinking bottle or pitcher should always be within sight. Also place healthy drinking water in the kitchen, preferably next to the refrigerator.

- Of course, a beautiful, classy looking vessel will help you drink. Plus, an appealing vessel gives you a positive mindset with which to enjoy every sip. This has a great effect on your health and well-being.

- Drink at least one glass of water before and after every meal and also with every cup of coffee.

- Always keep a full bottle of water in the car on long car trips.

- Always have a bottle of healthy water with you when you go to the theater or the movies.

- Always take a filled water bottle with you when you go to the gym.

- Provide variety: you can infuse your drinking water with peppermint leaves, ginger pieces, or a slice of lemon to give it a culinary kick.

- If you drink one or two glasses of healthy water on an empty stomach after getting up in the morning, your body will feel it immediately and will be grateful.

- Drinking a glass of water each night before going to bed speeds up falling asleep and ensures a deep and healthy sleep.

- You can keep a tally sheet (one tally for each glass of water) to keep track of how much you drink each day. Plus, there are now beepers that remind you to drink at irregular intervals.

- Important: The less you eat, the more you should drink to compensate for the lack of hydration from solid foods.

- Make sure you always have enough healthy water with you when you're on the go. Don't rely on having access to healthy water anywhere either.

- Ask yourself, no matter where you are (at work, at home, at the theater, at a workout, etc.), "Where's my water?"

ALWAYS ASK YOURSELF, "WHERE IS MY WATER?"

How much should you drink?

Paying attention to the amount of water you drink each day is important for optimal health. Fortunately, most people drink when they are thirsty, but most people have lost their natural thirst. According to the National Academies, 1 fl.oz. per kilogram (=2.2 lbs) of body weight is recommended. Accordingly, a person weighing 143 lbs. has a daily water requirement of just under 68 fl.oz., with about 20 percent of daily water intake coming from solid food. You should increase your water intake if you are physically active or live in a hotter region.

WATER AND AWARENESS

Awareness is the framework in which feelings unfold. Thoughts influence our emotional world and all our bodily functions. How water affects our body depends above all on our awareness.

Today we can experience our feelings about water together with two exercises.

Exercise 1:
Close your eyes and imagine yourself sitting in the tower restaurant of the most expensive hotel in the world. The view is breathtaking, a round table set exclusively for you.

A waiter pours water from a bottle into your glass. The price of the bottle of water is 2000 dollars. Supposedly water from the North Pole glacier. At the first sip, you now try to taste this special water. Is it fresher? Is it smoother? Is it sweeter? Yes, it tastes different, maybe even better. Now, as you continue to drink, you can become even more engaged with the water and perhaps find other positive aspects. Whether these justify the price, I will not be the judge.

Exercise 2:

You set out before sunrise to fetch water. You are now standing in front of a well in the middle of the desert, more than 100 meters deep. You lower a bucket into the depths on a rope. After the bucket is submerged in the water, you pull it back up - more than 200 times your hands must reach over until you have the bucket in your hands again.

Now you fill the bucket into a can, which you tie onto your back. Now you are on your way home: 30 kilometers and four hours lie ahead of you. You don't feel the ten kilos very much at first, but they get heavier and heavier the longer you walk. You arrive home just before sunset. You take down the can, grab a glass, sit on a bench and pour yourself some of the well water. When you take your first sip, you feel the dried buds on your tongue softening again, saliva forming in your oral cavity once more.

You feel every region in your mouth as the water flows past, gently sliding down your esophagus, cooling it, and arriving in your stomach. You register how the body surfaces become cooler and more moistened. Suddenly you have a sense of taste again and feel a sense of happiness that people rarely get to experience so intensely. The subsequent sips also seem like a blessing to you, and you appreciate each one as valuable and luck-bringing. Peace, relaxation and well-being now dominate your senses. If you now open your eyes again, you can let both impressions take effect on you.

Perhaps you now understand much better why Dr. Masaru Emoto claims that the effect of water on the body is influenced first and foremost by your own consciousness with which you drink water.

He talked to water, played music to water, informed it with writings, images or pure thought. As a result, the water showed new forms.

Dr. Emoto taught us that we can interact with water by informing it with the energy of words like Love, Peace, Gratititude, Health, etc. Likewise, water "informs" the water in our cells with live, energy and health. No matter how strong the impact of our words or attitude towards water is, this exercise does not take very much effort and can easily be repeated with every sip of water.

WE CAN INFLUENCE OUR CONSCIOUSNESS OURSELVES. IT CONTROLS OUR PERCEPTION AND THE EFFECT OF WATER ON OUR BODY.

SOBONFU SOMÉ

When I did research for this book, I went through my personal library of books on water and crystals. I came across a book that I had last read about 17 years ago. The title is "Of the essence of water". In this book, a very extraordinary and remarkable woman also wrote a chapter:

An awake spirit being who seemed full of agility and wanderlust, who aspired to set out for new realms and at the same time liked and wanted to protect nothing more than the old rituals. Her people gave her the name Sobonfu, "Guardian of Rituals". They could only survive because everything that makes this people, the rituals, their values and tradition has been passed down through each generation. For this generation Sobonfu was selected by the sages of the tribe. She was incorporated into the elders' association at a very young age. Sobonfu Somé was born and raised in Burkina Faso, Africa, in a settlement of 200 people called Dano. Among the Dagara, every newborn is considered a little teacher who is helped to find himself. In the case of Sobonfu, during the "ritual of listening," the elders encountered an extraordinary spirit, even before her birth.

I dedicate a chapter to her in my book because I was deeply impressed by her mindset. Now style-wise I have decided to present her teachings in the form of an interview, so her core teachings are much more concise to understand in my opinion.

Ewald:

Sobonfu, what motivates you to take on all the hardships to travel the world giving lectures?

Sobonfu:

The elders had in mind not only to preserve the old indigenous traditions, but to protect them in the long term through spreading them. Africa is so busy modernizing and increasingly rejecting all that is old. So my mission was to keep the old rituals alive - maybe not in Africa itself, but here in the West, where my people might be able to pick them up again someday.

Ewald:

Sobonfu, you grew up in a village in Africa, please describe your hometown.

Sobonfu:

In our small mud hut village, in the middle of dry area, there was very little, but I grew up in a loving security. Our daily struggle was the supply of water. Women and the children spent every day more than half of our time to fetch our drinking water. Care and love were constantly present with all of us.

Ewald:

How can I imagine the process of obtaining water?

Sobonfu:

We set out before the day began, walking for several hours to carry the water with a calabash (pumpkin shell) on our heads. Psychologically, carrying water in my tradition means not only being peaceful within with oneself, but carrying peace and reflecting it in all one's actions. When you drink water, it means not only that you flush impurities from your body, but that you supply energy to your soul, life energy. Any contact with water should be in a sacred manner, for water is sacred and should be honored as such. If we treat water with respect, we stay healthy.

Ewald:

What else does water mean to you?

Sobonfu:

When we look at our lives and we see that they are disrupted, it is time for us to consciously add water to our lives. And whoever understands water in this way will be helped. In our tradition, water stands for peace, reconciliation and harmony; from chaos comes clarity and insight. It is used in our culture in arguments. When someone rushes at you in anger, you put yourself in a peaceful state because you know that all that person lacks is water. In this case, we offer the angry person a glass of water; after that, the energy will change noticeably. Thus, we are able to create a peaceful climate at any time by adding water elements to our environment.

Ewald:
We in the West say, "Water is water, so what?"

Sobonfu:
I can understand that, when I was in the US for the first time, I saw water gushing out of a tap in the wall. I could not understand it and sent a picture of this situation to my grandfather. Yes, for you water is something commonplace, as self-evident as breathing, you have forgotten the importance and lost the appreciation. That is why I was sent into the world by my tribe to remind you again of what is most important, so that peace and love, caring and gratitude can return to the world of stress, hectic and greed. And the Holy Spirit of togetherness enters your souls. I challenge everyone to recognize the sacred in everyday life and to live by it.

Ewald:
How do you define the term "spirituality"?

Sobonfu:
The concept of spirituality has nothing religious about it, but means the closeness to the sacred in everyday life that has been lost in the modern world. In Africa, the spiritual resides just behind the profane. When the space for the hidden is opened in the ritual to penetrate everyday life, it shows itself. Then let the "Spirit" be everywhere, in every stone, in every dog and cat, in the trees and mountains, in the sky - Spirit is everywhere. It is the spiritual life force in each of these beings and things; the force that makes them unique and what they are.

Ewald:

For me, water as a therapy is mostly known in its external application, not so much as a spiritual treatment.

Sobonfu:

When you come to our people as a guest, the first thing you are offered is water. It symbolizes that you are facing people here who are friendly to you. If you do not accept it because perhaps it is not the cleanest, it will be taken as a sign that you have not come in peace, it does not have to be hostility or warlike intentions, but conflicts that torment you. My tribal brothers now want to find out why you are bearing conflicts. They will attempt to approach your conflicts with a water ritual and prepare you for forgiveness. While the conflicts are now being discussed together, a pitcher of water is placed in the center and water is offered once again at the end of the ceremony. So we have many rituals where we use water for therapy. When we have a water deficit, it also manifests itself in a psychological way. My tradition talks about restless and rushed people having a lack of water. So if you know someone who is easily annoyed or irritated. who can't sit still, we say; he lacks water. So the first thing we offer such people, even those who are aggressive towards us, is a glass of water. Water as a peacemaker. Water reminds us that we truly live with the Holy One.

Ewald:

Can you also tell us about far-reaching social problems caused by the shortage of water.

Sobonfu:

Yes, water shortage is creating a serious problem for our community because it is causing young people to leave and go to the city and the knowledge and wisdom of the elders is lost. And what happens to the young people who are often very naive and arrive in the big city? They come into contact with AIDS, then they come home when they are about to die

Ewald:

Do you have any other special message.

Sobonfu:

I think we should treat and preserve our water-bearing planet, our Earth, with care. Therefore, I wish that in all gatherings, whether religious, political or social, water should be at the very center. I have been to a few peace conferences and have always suggested placing a pitcher of water in the center. It brings something bigger to the group. The water helps to create peace. Water is a peacemaker in both large and small ways. Also that some people who live in abundance of water and sometimes waste it carelessly, imagine how there are places in this world where people have to fight for every sip of water. So that some may become humble and recognize and appreciate the importance and sacredness of water.

On January 15, 2017, Sobonfu Somé passed away after a prolonged illness. Thousands have experienced her in conferences, seminars and other gatherings. She gave everyone she met healing energy for their journey.

> *„Let peace begin - with me.“*

STONES
PRIMAL
ELEMENT
OF NATURE

There are many types of stones. Each stone is the result of a process that lasted millions of years and was formed in specific ways. A stone is a solid body consisting of minerals, volcanic glasses, or other stones (example: conglomerate, a sedimentary stone with portions of gravel and boulders). Depending on the conditions under which stones were formed, a distinction is made between igneous, metamorphic, and sedimentary stones.

DEPENDING ON THEIR FORMATION, THREE TYPES OF STONES CAN BE DISTINGUISHED

- Igneous stones (magmatites) are stones formed from magma and lava. While magma is the hot, liquid stone mass underneath the earth's surface, when magma reaches the light of day it turns into lava.

- Metamorphic stones (metamorphites) are also called transitional stones. Their formation is different: Under the influence of heat and/or high pressure conditions, already existing stones are transformed in such a way that new stones are formed. The characteristics of metamorphic stones are very diverse and striking; they range from schistosity (plate-like segregation), band-like inclusions of minerals in the stone (gneiss) to the crystalline structure of marble or quartzite.

- Sedimentary stones are also called depositional stones and are the result of deposition and consolidation of various stone-forming materials: Components of sedimentary stones are weathered, crushed stones and minerals, biogenic products such as shells of various shells, snails and other organisms. The process of sedimentation is comparatively "gentle", so that a number of fossils can very often be found in sedimentary stones. The most common sedimentary stones are limestone, chalk, travertine, sandstone and dolomite.

- Stone salt also belongs to the family of sedimentites. However, the formation differs from the other sedimentary stones: The stone salt was deposited when seawater evaporated in enclosed lagoons and became trapped in stone layers over time.

Interesting because of their effect on us humans are especially the so-called healing stones:

An important component of natural healing methods are healing crystals, which are very popular as jewelry or hand charms, or even as a supplement in water. Healing crystals are either gemstones or semi-precious stones, to which special healing effects are attributed.

There are more than 380 gemstones and semi-precious stones with positive effects. The meaning of the word healing crystal refers to the tradition of crystal healing, that certain crystals have the ability to exert a special effect on people or living beings. Not every stone has a positive effect. Healing crystals are stones whose special effects have been tested and passed down traditionally over many centuries.

MANY STONES HAVE A SIGNIFICANT HEALING EFFECT DUE TO THEIR STRUCTURE.

Crystal healing deals with the knowledge of the healing powers of gemstones, which has been observed for thousands of years in various cultures. Whether in Indian Ayurveda, in traditional Chinese medicine, the teachings of ancient Egypt or in the Middle Ages, healing crystals and their effects have been described and handed down many times. The most extensive records come from Hildegard of Bingen (1098-1179), who empirically studied herbs and healing crystals. She described her extensive methods and treatments in detail, and the documentations are an enormous wealth of knowledge in modern crystal healing and among naturopathic therapists.

How does the energy of a healing crystals work?

Energy is emitted from every object in the world. Every object, whether plant, animal, human or even an inanimate object such as a crystal, emits energy in the form of electromagnetic radiation or electromagnetic waves.

Every object receives its energies in the form of heat, food or light. Stones, as previously described, are formed under various conditions and have stored the energy that was present at the time of their formation (heat, pressure, water and light). In a crystal formed millions or billions of years ago, the energy supplied to it is conserved.

**ENERGY EMANATES FROM EVERY OBJECT
AND SENDS IT INTO ITS ENVIRONMENT.**

Each stone has the following types of information:

Basic information: Basic information is understood to be all the factors that cause certain substances to arrange and combine in such a way that this element can be created. Minerals or gemstones are not created by chance, very specific information conditions the composition to a very special natural product.

Origin information: Each stone undergoes specific processes of heating, pressure, concentration of various individual elements, decomposition and reformation. These processes give the stone a unique imprint with corresponding information that is preserved in the stone.

Structural information: Molecules strive to optimally fill the available space. This intention gives rise to certain patterns of order and structures that are inherent in a stone as typical information.

Substance Information: Every original substance and every compound contain their own information. This substance information is part of the stone and its basic peculiarities such as hardness, density transparency, cleavability etc.

Color information: Colors are parts of the light spectrum and have specific energy qualities. These influence physical, chemical and biological processes and also affect the mental and spiritual realm of all living beings. All manifestations of our nature, including stones, have unique color information.

HEALING CRYSTALS HAVE BEEN OUR CONSTANT COMPANIONS FOR CENTURIES.

These types of information within each stone create a characteristic energy that is released to the immediate environment. Energy like light and heat is a certain sequence of electromagnetic waves. It can be seen as light or heard as radio frequency, but there are other ranges of this spectrum that humans cannot perceive directly, such as ultraviolet light, radioactivity, etc. Stones also send this information in certain frequencies, which make each stone unique, and accordingly have an influence on us. Because like every object in the world, we are also receptive to energy.

The important characteristics of a healing crystal include the *mineral class, **crystal structure, formation, and color. Healing crystals, be they gemstones or precious stones, have a special effect on people due to their unique properties - more than other types of stones can do.

The essential conclusion is that a stone passes on its information to us. Information that the stone has absorbed and stored in the form of vibrations during its formation and existence, usually over millions of years. The quality of the information depends on various factors that make up a healing crystal:

- Special formation history (age, region, way of formation)
- Individual color or colors (rainbow spectrum and resonance with the chakras),
- Mineral Class*
- Crystal Structure**
- Blends and inclusions
- Shape (rough stone, tumbled stone, cut, disc, etc.)

*Mineral class, unit of the crystal-chemical classification of minerals. Since minerals are primarily crystalline and are formed by chemical reactions, they are divided into nine classes:

- Sulfides
- HalogenidOxides
- Carbonates (nitrates)
- Borade
- Sulphade
- Phosphate
- Silicates
- Organic minerals

** In the course of their formation, stones form their fundamental atomic structure. This is called crystal structure. This refers to the 7 geometric shapes that are able to fill an existing space without gaps:

- Cubical
- Hexagonal
- Trigonal
- Tetragonal
- Rhombic
- Monacolin
- Triclinic
- Amorphous

The use of "healing crystals" is neither a therapy nor a diagnosis in the medical sense. The use of healing crystals should in no way replace medical advice, but should only serve to support a therapy.

> „You can break a stone, but
> you can't take away its effect.“
>
> — Lü Bu We

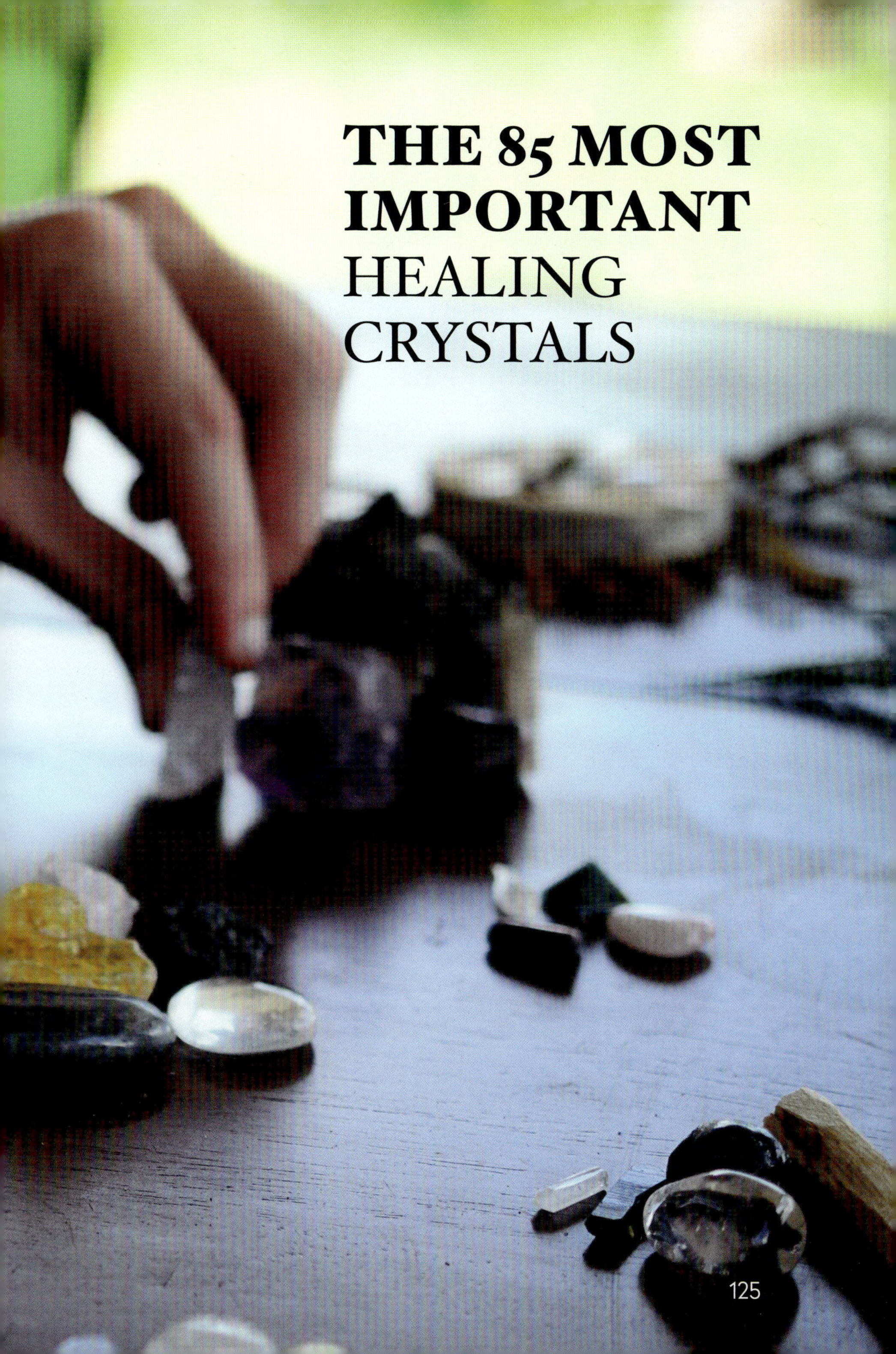

THE 85 MOST
IMPORTANT
HEALING
CRYSTALS

Explanation for the following pages:

Some stones are attributed special properties to the hour of birth. The zodiac symbols at the bottom of the description show the particular suitability of the gemstone in relation to the zodiac sign.

In Hinduism, also in Yoga, Chakra (Sanskrit for "wheel" or "circle") refers to the assumed original energy centers between the physical body and the ethereal body of the human being. In the symbols at the bottom you will find the significant relationship of the gemstone to the respective chakra:

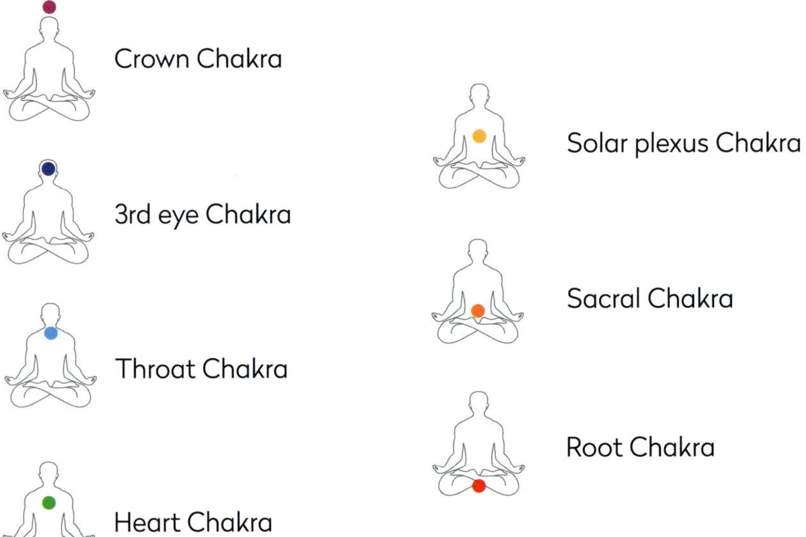

At the bottom you will find additional symbols
for the use of gemstones:

Can be used as jewelry

Can be placed on the body

Can be used as a hand charm

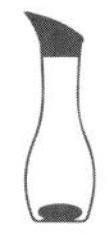

Can be used for crystal water

> *„God decided not to end the shine*
> *and the power of the gemstones,*
> *intending them to be valued and*
> *praised and be used for healing on Earth."*
>
> — Hildegard von Bingen —

AGATE

SERENITY
CONFIDENCE

SIGNIFICANCE

Agate is a banded stone and belongs to the group of chalcedony quartz. It belongs to the mineral class of oxides. In ancient times, it was considered a lucky charm and protective stone that every Egyptian carried with him. Agate promotes serenity and humor, calmness and self-confidence.

EFFECT ON THE BODY

It helps with stomach ailments, fever and eye ailments. It is also said to have a supportive effect for a healthy pregnancy. Furthermore, it is used with sleep disorders. It supports the strengthening of cell tissue and blood vessels. Its current applications are also related to the beauty sector, because it provides a better and purer skin.

EFFECT ON PSYCHE

It offers relief from grief in separations, it stops sleepwalking. Agate can increase overall vitality, boost self-confidence, and thus prevent depression. With agate, many feel protected from negative energies and have an overall sense of relief.

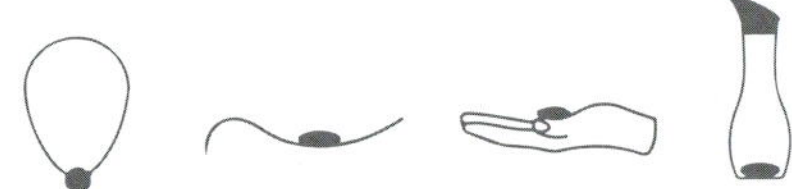

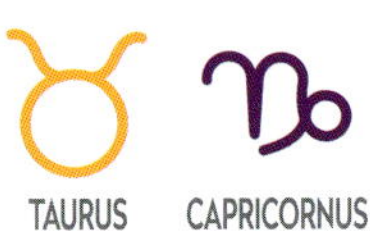

AMAZONITE

ENCOURAGEMENT
ALLOW LIFE TO FLOW

SIGNIFICANCE

Amazonite is an opaque potassium feldspar, mostly formed by large triclinic crystals metamorphic. Amazonite fills with positive energy and cleanses the heart chakra of negativity so that love can take its place. It is often called a lucky hope stone.

EFFECT ON THE BODY

Amazonite helps relieve pain in the solar plexus area and works against heart problems caused by stress and agitation. It has a relaxing and calming effect on the entire body. Relieves tension in the back and neck areas. Helps against stress, hectic, restlessness, tension and cramps.

EFFECT ON PSYCHE

Amazonite has a balancing effect and soothes mood swings. It can bring patience as well as tolerance and dissolve discord, disagreement, learning difficulties, stinginess as well as selfishness. In this way, it can also help with grief or sadness, give more joy in life as well as vitality and improve the interaction of mind and intuition. Overnight, it can help you get a soothing sleep when placed under the pillow and keep nightmares away.

AQUARIS

AMBER

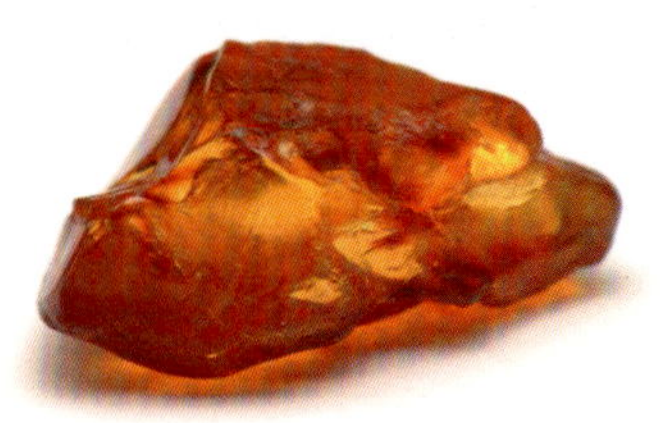

LOVE FOR LIFE
OPTIMISM,
CREATIVITY

SIGNIFICANCE

Amber does not belong to any mineral class, as it is neither a stone nor a mineral. Nevertheless, it is counted among the precious stone. It is a fossil tree resin up to 260 million years old. Above all, it is known as the stone of zest for life and optimism. It calms the mind and can relieve depression and anxiety. It awakens the spirits and provides creative ideas.

EFFECT ON THE BODY

Amber soothes eczema, pimples, warts, dandruff and herpes. It can also be used for the throat and neck area as well as for hay fever and pollen allergies. Everyone surely knows the use of amber as a dental aid for babies. Other uses are for inflammation of the mouth and throat, for arthritis, gout, rheumatism, and to support the body's immune defenses. Here, the use of an amber crystal water has proven particularly effective. Supposed to prevent tick bites.

EFFECT ON PSYCHE

It has a positive influence on the state of mind, helps with depression, strengthens self-confidence, promotes flexibility, open-mindedness and creativity. It is an inspiring sunstone that inspires zest for life. It strengthens decisiveness and helps with cluelessness and depression. It brings light and warmth to the mind and brings a fresh and cheerful aura.

AMETHYST

INTUITION
RELAXATION
INNER PEACE

SIGNIFICANCE

Amethyst is a purple variety of quartz. It crystallizes from ferrous silica and belongs to the mineral class of oxides. This stone strengthens concentration and is excellent for meditation. It strengthens the will, gives joy, courage and comfort, promotes intuition, relaxation, inner peace and confidence in oneself.

EFFECT ON THE BODY

Amethyst has a pain-relieving effect. Migraines and headaches are said to be positively influenced by the stone, especially if they are caused by weather sensitivity and tension. Likewise, the stone is said to be beneficial for skin diseases. Other fields of application are insect and snake bites, swellings and bruises, inflammations, sore throats and itching.

EFFECT ON PSYCHE

Amethyst is said to have purifying powers. It is believed to drive away superfluous and burdensome thoughts and strengthen concentration. Inner peace, coupled with calm and serenity, is what many people are looking for today. This stone should help to find and keep these feelings again. In addition, amethyst is said to dissolve blockages and inhibitions.

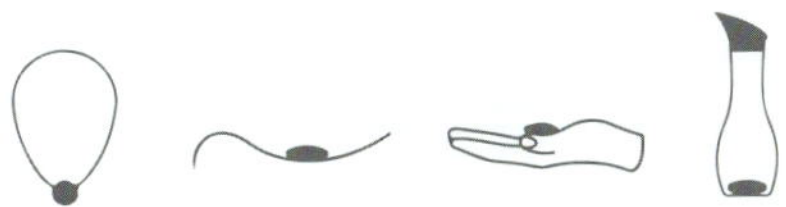

VIRGO

AMETRINE

CALMNESS
OPTIMISM
CREATIVITY

SIGNIFICANCE

Ametrine is a variety of quartz, it belongs to the mineral class of oxides. It has a particularly relaxing effect on the soul and emotional life, bringing them back into harmonious balance. It brings about serenity as well as inner peace, awakens zest for life and can help with nervousness or lack of drive. Ametrine supports an optimistic mindset.

EFFECT ON THE BODY

Physically, the ametrine has a strong cleansing effect and balances the interaction of all organs. It is beneficial for the nervous system and stimulates the metabolism. Ametrine activates the brain, harmonizes the brain waves of both sides and stimulates oxygenation. The stone supports the activity of the autonomic nervous system and is used for nervous digestive disorders. It supports the purification and regeneration of all cells and tissues.

EFFECT ON PSYCHE

Ametrine is effective against stress, nervousness, and depression. It is half amethyst and half citrine, so it has a particularly soothing effect on our soul. The ametrine helps to combine apparent opposites and leads to well-considered, confident action. It stimulates optimism and joie de vivre, creativity and inner well-being.

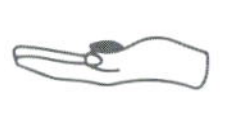

ANGELITE

GROUNDING
SECURITY
STABILITY

SIGNIFICANCE

Angelite forms in sediments from evaporated seawater and belongs to the mineral class of sulfates. Angelite gives inner stability as well as security and helps during extraordinary stress. At the same time, it helps to be more down to earth. Angelite can also be used to help against schizophrenia.

EFFECT ON THE BODY

Angelite relieves throat problems, it regulates kidney function and stimulates the internal balance of water distribution in the body. It reduces water accumulation in the tissues, so-called oedemas, and the associated swelling.

EFFECT ON PSYCHE

In crystal healing, Angelite is considered as a helper against mental strain, stress and insecurity. It should provide peace and relaxation and stimulates patience. It brings about stability, security and gives confidence in oneself. Supports a rational approach in psychologically tense and unbalanced phases of life, has a stabilizing effect in cases of extreme psychological stress.

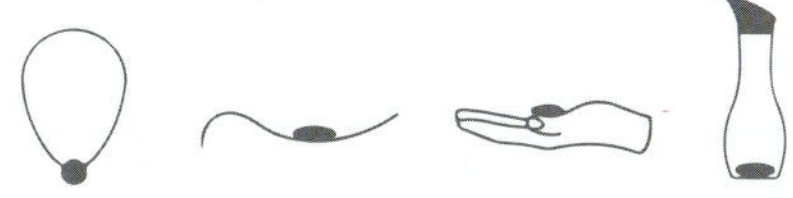

APATITE

FIND YOUR OWN PATH

SIGNIFICANCE

The apatite crystal is a combination of different amounts of fluorine, chlorine and hydroxide. It brings motivation, optimism, determination and flexibility to make life more versatile. It also stimulates mental development and independence, gives new self-confidence and helps to get rid of inhibitions.

EFFECT ON THE BODY

Apatite helps against apathy, fatigue or lack of drive. Boosts activity, digestion and metabolism. Has a cleansing energy, strengthens the immune system and is an indispensable helper in the flu season. It also strengthens muscle tissue and helps with digestive problems.

EFFECT ON PSYCHE

Provides clarity of mind to distinguish the important from the unimportant. Brings motivation, optimism, determination as well as flexibility to make life more diversified and give it a new zest. It also stimulates mental development and independence, and brings openness and sociability.

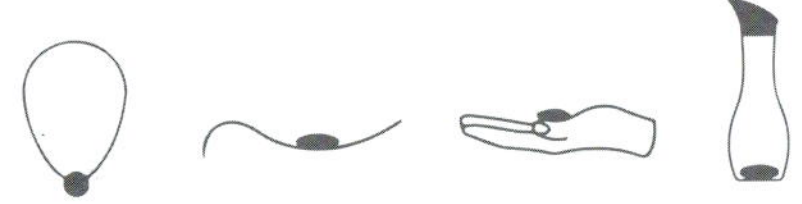

AQUAMARINE

TRANQUILITY
ANTI STRESS

SIGNIFICANCE

Aquamarine consists of the rare mineral beryllium. It is a symbol of youth and eternal happiness. Aquamarine helps to clear the mind and balance emotions. It brings a calming energy and helps to bring peace, tranquility and serenity to an overactive mind.

EFFECT ON THE BODY

It has a positive effect on our glands, protects against senility and forgetfulness. Improves vision, helps with allergies (especially hay fever) and is an important stone in all diseases of the respiratory tract. The stone harmonizes the hormonal balance of the thyroid and lymph glands. Helps with toothache, liver and stomach diseases, protects against colds and strengthens the immune system.

EFFECT ON PSYCHE

Working with the high vibrational forces of aquamarine reduces the influence of doubt and negativity. It washes away negativity, strengthens intuitive powers and awareness to enable honest and articulate communication. It gives not only foresight and prudence, but also perseverance. In this way, it gives resilience and helps to finish what you have started.

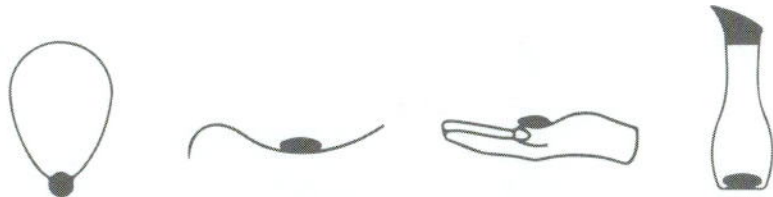

AVENTURINE

OPTIMISM
POSITIVITY

SIGNIFICANCE
Aventurine is a quartz and belongs to the mineral class of oxides. Its random inclusions of fuchsite gives it its green color. It is characterized by the iridescence of the enclosed mineral platelets, which is also known as aventurizing. It gives optimism, which makes getting out of your comfort zone less frightening. It also provides relaxation, recreation and a positive attitude towards life.

EFFECT ON THE BODY
It has a positive effect on the heart area and stimulates the regeneration of this organ, stimulates metabolism, reduces flatulence, bloating, constipation and diarrhea. Helps against skin allergies, eczema, rashes, neurodermatitis. Has a positive effect on hair and connective tissue. Green aventurine helps with hair loss, dandruff, split ends and brittle hair.

EFFECT ON PSYCHE
Aventurine brings relaxation, recreation and a positive attitude towards life. It stimulates self-determination as well as an individual personality, gives inner balance and frees us from worries, fears or psychosomatic disorders. In addition, aventurine relieves stress as well as nervousness, stimulates positive dreams and gives cheerfulness as well as humor.

AZURITE

FOCUS
WISDOM
MENTAL EXPANSION

SIGNIFICANCE

Azurite is a copper carbonate from the mineral class of carbonates. However, pseudo-morphism can occur when azurite absorbs water. The color of azurite is determined by the copper that it contains. This stone helps to find focus by protecting the mind from any internal or external distractions.

EFFECT ON THE BODY

Azurite is considered a supporting stone for bones and joints in crystal healing. It guides, regulates and stimulates healthy growth, which is understandably important, especially for children and adolescents. It stimulates brain and nervous activity, has a detoxifying effect and supports the work of the liver, it also reduces inflammation. A stone for arthritis, spinal curvature and spleen complaints, which strengthens joints and bones and strengthens the circulation.

EFFECT ON PSYCHE

The azure blue azurite increases concentration and strengthens the sense of righteousness. It makes you more critical and makes you think about things that were previously considered normal. Through this, opinions and thought patterns can be changed or decisions can be made easier. It also makes you more receptive, insightful and self-confident, and allows you to think through courses of action more thoroughly.

CAPRICORNUS

BLOODSTONE (HEMATITE)

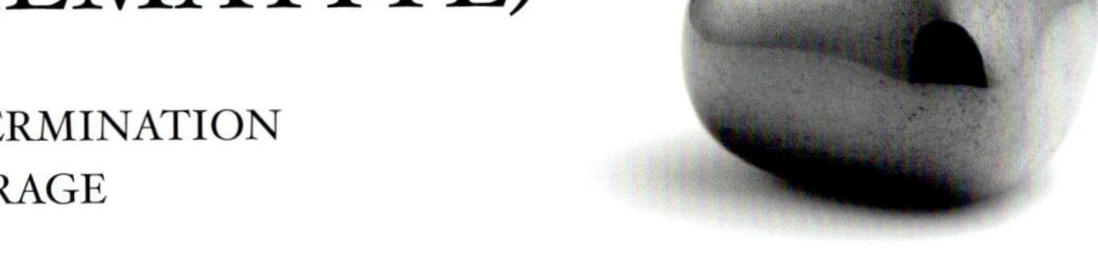

DETERMINATION
COURAGE

SIGNIFICANCE

Hematite is the most common naturally occurring form of iron oxide, it belongs to the mineral class of oxides. Hematite brings courage and gives vitality and zest for life. Through more spontaneity, independence, relaxation and determination, one's own needs receive more attention. Hematite thereby contributes to the improvement of the quality of life.

EFFECT ON THE BODY

Hematite helps the blood circulation, supports blood purification, promotes cell and blood building, strengthens the liver and helps against iron deficiency. Hematite therefore also has the name "bloodstone". It stimulates the formation of blood and ensures faster resolution of bleeding and bruising. Strengthens liver, spleen, lungs and kidneys; stimulates recovery; stimulates wound closure and healing.

EFFECT ON PSYCHE

It boosts dynamism and vitality, activates the willpower and drive. Hematite gifts us with more spontaneity and zest for life. It builds a protective field around us and thereby enables us to live more courageously, carefree and purposefully. Mental spasms are relieved with the help of hematite, especially hematite roses.

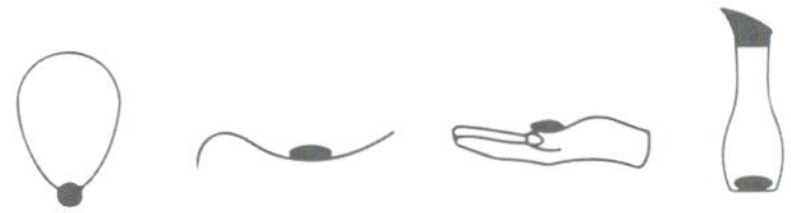

CALCITE

ADVANCED DEVELOPMENT
MENTAL STRENGTH

SIGNIFICANCE

Calcite is a stone -forming mineral and is one of the most abundant minerals in the world. As calcium carbonate, it belongs to the mineral class of carbonates. Calcite stimulates mental development, brings creativity and strengthens memory. By having a positive effect on the ability to think, it also increases self-confidence and gives steadfastness.

EFFECT ON THE BODY

Calcite stimulates the metabolism and strengthens the immune system. The healing crystal benefits the blood clotting. It is particularly suitable for healing muscle tissue, skin, teeth and bones. It strengthens the heart and serves as a prophylaxis against intervertebral disc problems. Calcite supports the entire throat and pharynx and has a detoxifying effect on the entire organism.

EFFECT ON PSYCHE

Calcite accelerates mental development, strengthens drive and memory, stimulates self-confidence and steadfastness, calmness and composure. It especially reinforces our self-confidence and strengthens the cerebrum. It makes us look positively into the future thanks to its life-affirming effect and separates us from rigid thoughts.

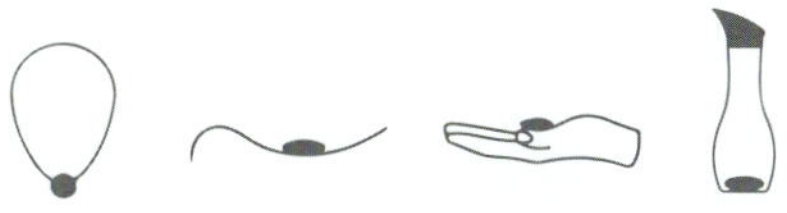

CARNELIAN

CREATIVITY,
MOTIVATION
TRUST

SIGNIFICANCE

Carnelian is a variety of chalcedony and thus a very fine-grained quartz. It belongs to the mineral class of oxides. It gives steadiness, courage and drive, not only lifts the spirits, but also helps to face challenges or overcome problems through solution-oriented thinking. It supports helpfulness and idealism. Carnelian restores vitality and a zest for life.

EFFECT ON THE BODY

Carnelian stimulates digestion, metabolism, strengthens the intestines, liver, abdomen and blood circulation. Good for detoxification. It can be used against blood impurities, rheumatism, hay fever, nosebleeds. It stops bleeding, strengthens the spleen, strengthens the immune system, supports the function of the stomach, intestines, liver and kidneys, helps with periodontal disease and bleeding gums, has a general regulating and stimulating effect.

EFFECT ON PSYCHE

Carnelian gives courage and drive through its iron components, it gives decisiveness where commitment and spirited action are required. As an oxide, it succeeds in transforming uncertain, open situations into stable, clarified ones. This crystal is all about vibrancy, from its color to its energy. It helps to break free from the norm and awakens the desire for adventure. Gives a bold, new perspective to tackle life in a fresh way.

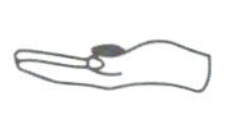

CELESTINE

BALANCE
CONFIDENCE
JOY

SIGNIFICANCE

Celestine usually forms as void fillings, it belongs to the mineral class of sulfates. It brings body and soul in harmony and thus gives more joy, relaxation and balance. Gives confidence and drive and relieves anxiety.

EFFECT ON THE BODY

Celestine is an effective (wound) healing crystal and is popular for use in injuries and surgeries. It accelerates the recovery of injured tissues, also relieves headaches, helps against tension and refreshes the eyes.

EFFECT ON PSYCHE

Celestine leads to a harmonious balance with the environment and contributes to an improved sense of well-being. It ensures a good flow of energy and thus strengthens the personal charisma. Celestine can also be used against anxiety and internal blockages. Helps you to gradually feel more secure in the world again, personal anxiety disappears.

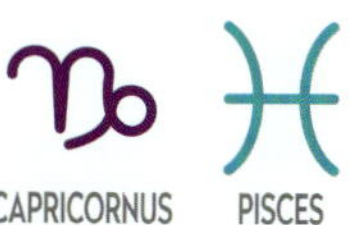

CHALCEDONY

RHETORIC
STRESS REDUCTION
CALMNESS

SIGNIFICANCE

Chalcedony is a fibrous microcrystalline quartz and belongs to the mineral class of oxides. This stone relieves stress and puts you in a calmer state of mind. Helps to express oneself rhetorically in a convincing way.

EFFECT ON THE BODY

Chalcedony helps with disorders in the lungs and respiratory tract, but also in the throat and pharynx. It is popularly called "orator stone" because it gives a strong, melodious voice to people who have to speak, recite or even sing a lot. Effective against sore throat, cough, hoarseness, nervousness, stuttering, hormonal disorders (menopause). It helps with fever, festering wounds and against varicose veins. Supports the formation of red blood cells.

EFFECT ON PSYCHE

This stone is wonderful for those who have difficulty expressing themselves for fear of criticism. The connection to the chalcedony releases the throat chakra and strengthens the love of truth. The energy of this stone helps you to express yourself more authentically. It also strengthens rhetoric, gives self-confidence and can release inhibitions or anxiety. Blue chalcedony can prevent melancholy, insomnia and nightmares.

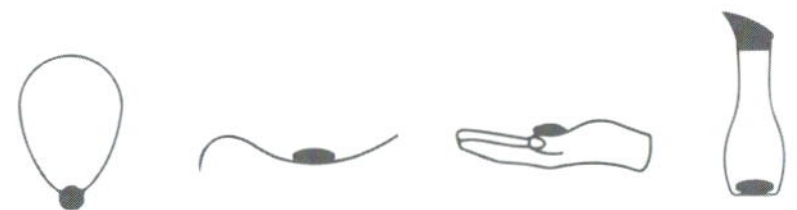

CHRYSOCOLLA

WELL-BEING
BALANCE

SIGNIFICANCE

Chrysocolla is a copper mineral that belongs to the class of silicates. The green stone of hope works well against stress and brings personal balance. Its energies stimulate both the well-being and the mental state. It promotes inner peace and gives more serenity.

EFFECT ON THE BODY

Chrysocolla soothes the stomach. In phases when the hormonal balance fluctuates, this healing crystal can provide good support for the body. Therefore, women in particular prefer to use the mineral.

EFFECT ON PSYCHE

Chrysocolla harmonizes the personal charisma. It helps to find a firm hold within oneself. Overcomes states of inner restlessness and achieves more serenity. Strengthens inner perception in conflicts and in relationship crises and in this way provides a good overview of the current life situation

CHRYSOPRASE

LOVE
OPENS THE HEART CHAKRA

SIGNIFICANCE

Chrysoprase belongs to the quartzes and as nickel containing chalcedony it is a mineral of the oxide class. It opens and activates the heart chakra, which allows a strong flow of healing energy to the heart. Helps with grief and can strengthen the heart. It gifts peace, security and confidence, provides new ways of thinking and gives hope.

EFFECT ON THE BODY

Chrysoprase is a stone for cleansing and detoxification. These intensive cleansing properties have a positive effect on the heart, blood and circulatory system. Chrysoprase gemstone elixir is used to support skin disorders such as neurodermatitis and fungal infections. It regulates blood pressure, prevents venereal diseases and promotes potency as well as fertility.

EFFECT ON PSYCHE

In ancient times, chrysoprase was considered a cure for depression. It brings peace, security, confidence, and provides new ways of thinking and gives hope. New paths in life can be mastered better with the help of chrysoprase, burdens from the past are better processed. Chrysoprase gives more fidelity, counteracts jealousy and helps with relationship problems.

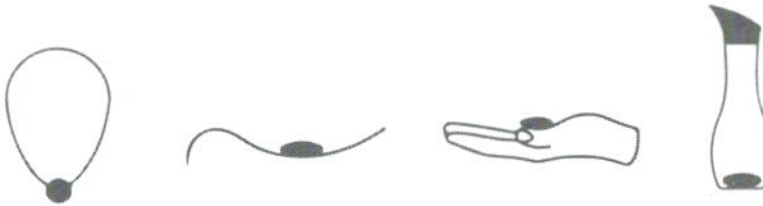

CITRINE

HAPPINESS
POSITIVITY

SIGNIFICANCE

Citrine is a yellow quartz and belongs to the mineral class of oxides. Citrine brings sunshine into life. Its radiant energy stimulates positivity, growth and abundance. It is one of the few crystals that does not store negativity and it fills the soul with happiness and light.

EFFECT ON THE BODY

Citrine not only helps with digestive problems, but also stimulates blood circulation, strengthens vision, stimulates the thymus gland, alleviates thyroid problems, has a stimulating and warming effect on any sensitivity to cold, strengthens the nerves, boosts the function of the stomach, spleen and pancreas, and relieves diabetes in its early stages. It also helps toddlers who often have tummy aches really well.

EFFECT ON PSYCHE

Citrine is a clarifying stone. Ambitious and decisive people will be helped to find the career track and to pass exams with success. It promotes concentration and stamina, strengthens self-confidence. Increases the joy of life, helps with stress and anxiety. Citrine is a pick-me-up that helps you get out of bed in the morning.

CLEAR QUARTZ

CLARITY

INSIGHT

INTUITION

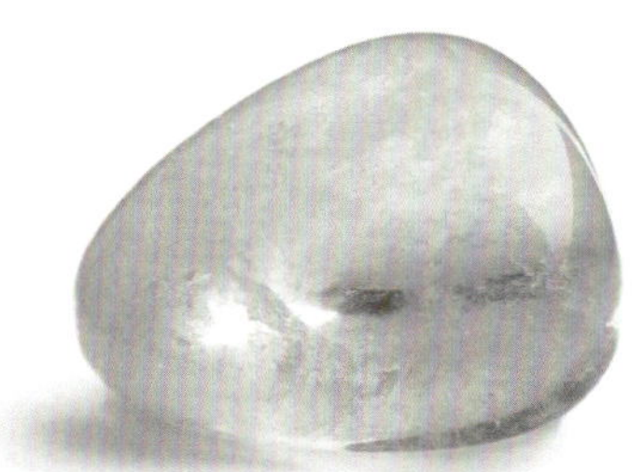

SIGNIFICANCE

Clear Quartz is quartz in its purest form and forms hydrothermally during cooling and crystallization. It has always been considered a stone of clarity and knowledge, whose effect is perceived by all cultures as particularly positive. The larger the stone, the more powerful its effect. It should be applied directly to the appropriate parts of the body or consumed as mountain crystal water.

EFFECT ON THE BODY

Hildegard von Bingen described the special importance of Clear Quartz in the treatment of ulcers, eye ailments and heart and stomach disorders. It has an effect on many organs and is used wherever purification and calming are required. Clear Quartz helps to reactivate numb or insensitive parts of the body. It gently regulates the blood circulation and regenerates the nervous system.

EFFECT ON PSYCHE

Clear Quartz stimulates the development of personality, gently gives strength and energy. It is a stone that conveys good thoughts and gentle power and acts on the entire body, harmoniously dissolves blockages in all areas. Instills clear and calm thinking. It causes the development of more attention and sensitivity in the relationship.

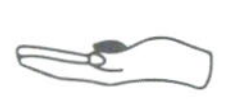

CORAL

LOVE FOR LIFE
PROTECTION
COMMUNITY SENSE

SIGNIFICANCE

Corals are the calciferous skeleton of cnidarians, so they belong to the mineral class of carbonates. The coral has always been considered a protective stone against all evil and negative energies. Provides vitality, joy and energy. It strengthens the personality and relieves anxiety and psychological or social tensions. It stimulates the need for love, partnership and friendship.

EFFECT ON THE BODY

Corals are overall very sensitive, they have a positive effect on hematopoiesis, and protect against infections. Have a supportive and calming effect on circulatory problems. Reduce circulatory disorders and act against hypertension. In older people they prevent bone fragility. Red coral has a very good effect on the enzymes in the stomach and liver that contribute to blood formation, therefore it prevents nutritional deficiencies.

EFFECT ON PSYCHE

Coral strengthens the ability to love and the need for partnership and friendship, makes one less likely to have envy and resentment. Corals have had a special effect on our spiritual life for thousands of years. As a protective stone, they store energy, joy and vitality.

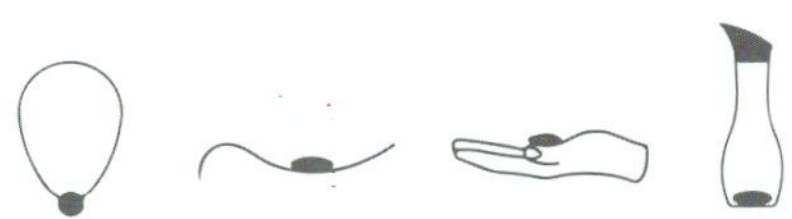

DIAMOND

CLARITY

SPIRITUAL ELEVATION

SIGNIFICANCE

Diamond is pure carbon that crystallizes at great depths under immense heat and pressure. It embodies invincibility and purity. The diamond transmits these values and gives strength of character, will-power and self-confidence. The diamond also conveys the urge for spiritual freedom, and is a symbol of purity and clear thoughts.

EFFECT ON THE BODY

It is the most curative stone and helps with headaches, back and limb pain, intervertebral disc problems and with strokes. Strengthens the brain and nerves, prevents calcification and senility, has a strengthening effect on all organs and body functions. Of all stones, it has the greatest healing power in the case of a stroke. The diamond frees us from blockages, sediments and impurities. Medicinal water, drunk in the morning on an empty stomach, dissolves kidney and gall stones.

EFFECT ON PSYCHE

It helps to consistently implement what one has recognized as right and important, strengthens wisdom and insight, but also conveys respect and esteem. Diamond is the guardian of the mind and supports clear and independent thinking, encourages mental heights. It is the stone of truth, loyalty to the overriding principle, promotes logical thinking. It helps us to look for the right path in life, to find it and to follow it.

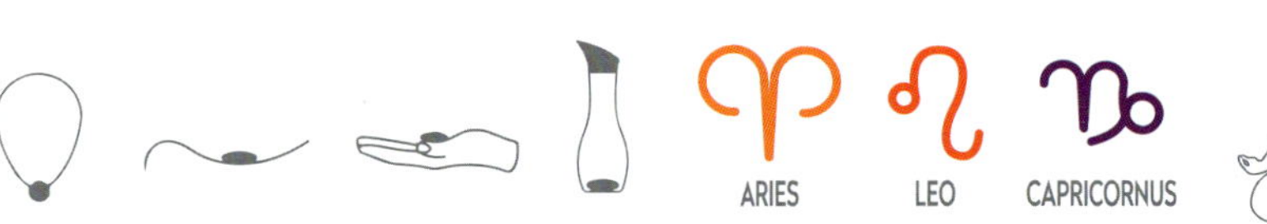

DISTHENE

IDENTITY
INTUITIVE THINKING

SIGNIFICANCE

Disthene is formed during stone metamorphism in aluminum-rich sediments, it belongs to the mineral class of silicates. Disthene strengthens one' s own identity. It allows for rational and also intuitive thinking and thus helps to calm one's nerves in chaotic situations. It has a supportive effect on resignation, improves articulation and helps with learning new languages.

EFFECT ON THE BODY

Physically, the stone has a good influence on the neck in particular. Like chalcedony, it is a good companion for singers and speakers. It relieves hoarseness and sore throats. Has a relaxing effect on speech disorders. It stimulates the learning of foreign languages. It strengthens the speech center and helps us find the right words.

EFFECT ON PSYCHE

Disthene stands for peace and serenity, freed from heavy burden and inner constraints. It stimulates calm nerves, clear pronunciation and concentration. It is a protective stone for the voice and can be used together with chalcedony. Recommended for teachers, salesmen, actors, singers and politicians, etc.

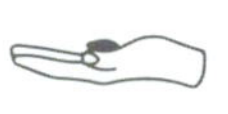

DOLOMITE

CONTENTMENT
SELF-REALIZATION

SIGNIFICANCE

Dolomite is formed by the interaction of magnesium-containing solutions with limestone. It belongs to the mineral class of carbonates. Dolomite stimulates self-realization, brings joy, promotes a positive and contented attitude to life and brings one closer to one's own desires. It balances the mind and helps with emotional outbursts.

EFFECT ON THE BODY

Dolomite helps with sore muscles, stomach and intestinal problems, has a relaxing and cramp-relieving effect and supplies the lungs and cells with oxygen. It also helps with cramps, is beneficial for the circulation and the heart. Dolomite regulates the metabolism, especially the balance of acids and bases, and is therefore a good remedy for heartburn.

EFFECT ON PSYCHE

Dolomite enhances self-realization, stabilizes and calms extreme emotional outbursts. It expresses sensual pleasures, helps to find one's place in life and in the community. It gives a balanced, peaceful temperament and balances intense emotions and anger. If you hold a grudge, it helps with forgiveness. Provides mental flexibility and openness, expands horizons.

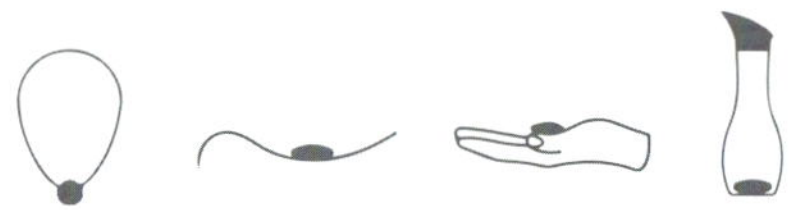

DUMORTIERITE

CONCENTRATION
STRESS REDUCTION
PATIENCE

SIGNIFICANCE

Dumortierite forms from magma. As an aluminum silicate, it belongs to the mineral class of silicates. It helps with anxiety or stress and strengthens the nerves, gives confidence and courage in difficult situations in life, brings inner peace and harmony, provides relaxation and balance.

EFFECT ON THE BODY

Dumortierite assists in addiction therapies, helps with diseases of the nerves and nervous system, relieves nervous headaches, nausea, vomiting, cramps, colic and diarrhea. Through its control of the glandular system, e.g. the thyroid gland, it ensures balance there. Water retention is reduced. It has fever reducing properties.

EFFECT ON PSYCHE

Dumortierite generally helps to increase concentration in everyday life. It enhances inner balance and helps to achieve more calmness. Through this stone, frequent stressful situations of everyday life (manager syndrome) are reduced, a deeper phase of relaxation occurs. This stone can reduce hyperactivity and stubbornness, gives perseverance and patience, brings courage and confidence, stimulates harmony and trust and dissolves fears.

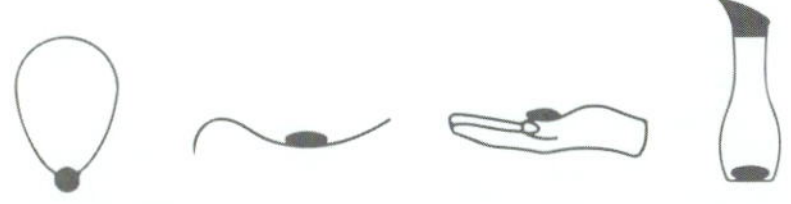

SAGITTARIUS

EMERALD

DIVINE INSPIRATION
INNER PEACE
HOPE

SIGNIFICANCE

Emerald is a variety of beryl. It belongs to the mineral class of silicates. Emerald has always stood for beauty, harmony and justice. It brings back mental balance and clarity. It can help overcome life crises. As a stone of "divine inspiration", it gives rise to new ideas and flashes of inspiration.

EFFECT ON THE BODY

Emerald activates the self-healing powers, rejuvenates and regenerates. It is said to have strong healing powers even in severe diseases. In heart disease, kidney disorders, diabetes, gastrointestinal diseases, infections, rheumatism, gout, headaches, children's diseases and eye diseases, you can safely use an emerald. Its chromium content has a detoxifying, liver stimulating, and deacidifying effect.

EFFECT ON PSYCHE

The emerald creates inner balance and more harmony. It leads to satisfaction and more joy in life. The emerald is characterized by social competence and striving for harmony as well as love of truth and aesthetics. It represents vision and artistic inspiration. Its swing and verve helps against indecisiveness. Emerald is a fighter for harmony, but also for justice.

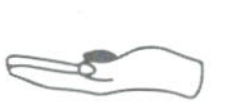

CANCER   LIBRA

EPIDOTE

RESILIENCE
RELAXATION
SELF-CONFIDENCE

SIGNIFICANCE

Epidote forms hydrothermally by metasomatosis (exchange of stone types) and is a compound of calcium, iron and aluminum. Epidote increases resilience, has a relaxing effect and gives more self-reliance. In addition, it brings hope as well as patience and helps with self-pity, resignation or grief.

EFFECT ON THE BODY

Also called unakite, epidote provides a sense of balance and strengthens the functions of all organs. Boosts the efficiency of the glands and their bodily fluids. The characteristic healing effect of this stone lies in its relaxing and decramping effect on the lower genital area in both men and women.

EFFECT ON PSYCHE

In the psychological aspect, epidote has very balancing properties. It especially alleviates problems that have settled within us due to an improper upbringing in our childhood years. Women, who have a psychological aversion to men due to earlier negative experiences, are brought back to more harmonious levels of life and sexuality with the help of the epidote. It strengthens mental resilience, especially in crisis situations.

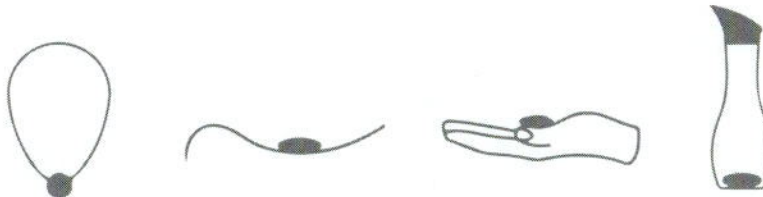

FIRE OPAL

SPONTANEITY
NEW IDEAS
ENTHUSIASM

SIGNIFICANCE

Fire opal is formed as cavity filling in volcanic stones, it belongs to the mineral class of oxides. With the help of fire opal, "fire" can be brought back into one's sexual activity . It increases spontaneity, allows room for new ideas. Due to its uplifting effect, fire opal is able to give new zest for life as well as enthusiasm again.

EFFECT ON THE BODY

Fire opal helps very well with disorders of the digestive tract. It stabilizes the blood circulation, supports the elasticity of the blood vessels and reduces deposits in the vessels. It is the first choice for weakness and dizziness, has a restorative and stabilizing effect.

EFFECT ON PSYCHE

Fire opal stands for strength, energy, creativity, vitality and joy. It is the stone of sensual pleasure. It increases the pleasure of sexuality in women and the potency of men. It brings more zest for life, boosts hormone production and thus makes us more "energetic". Thus, new horizons develop, which can be realized more easily and with greater momentum with fire opal. It guards against mood swings and gives the body strength and vitality.

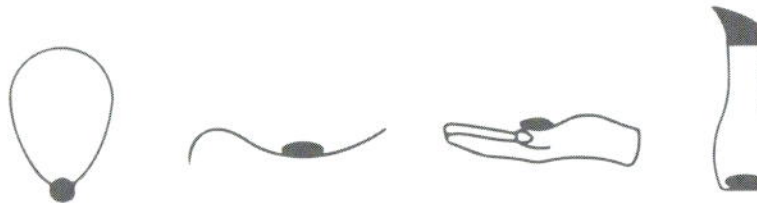

FLUORITE

INTUITION
CREATIVITY
MINDFULNESS

SIGNIFICANCE

Pure fluorite is colorless, it is mostly formed primarily during cooling by magma and belongs to the mineral class of halides. Fluorite helps with learning difficulties and is particularly suitable as a healing crystal for concentration and learning difficulties, it increases receptivity and creativity. Reduces restrictive lifestyles and enhances intuition.

EFFECT ON THE BODY

Fluorite stimulates the regeneration of skin and mucous membrane cells, heals pimples and wounds, clears the respiratory tract and is successfully used for allergies that have a psychological origin. It has a strong influence on bone formation and helps with osteoarthritis and osteoporosis. The healing of injuries, strengthening of lungs and liver are other areas of application.

EFFECT ON PSYCHE

Fluorite stabilizes the psyche, provides more flexibility, favors the perceptive faculty, sensitizes the intuitive sensations, strengthens concentration. Due to its strong inspirational effect, it stimulates receptivity, intuition and concentration. During exams, fluorite takes away test anxiety.

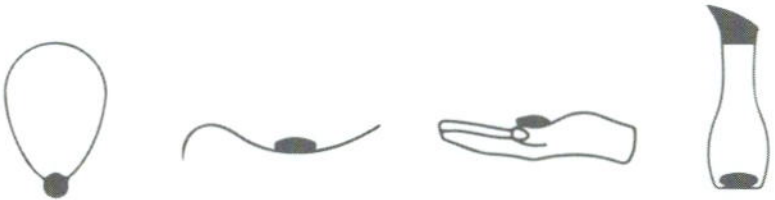

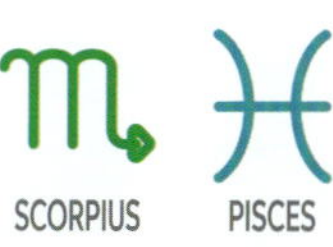

FUCHSITE

PERSPECTIVE
SOVEREIGNTY
SOLUTION FOCUSED

SIGNIFICANCE

As mica, fuchsite belongs to the mineral class of silicates. Fuchsite can be helpful as a protective stone for depression, anxiety and melancholy. It also lends a confident presence in difficult situations. He helps to find new perspectives in order to find good solutions. Likewise, it strengthens the senses and makes one calmer and more sovereign. It stimulates creativity.

EFFECT ON THE BODY

Fuchsite provides a harmonious balance of red and white blood cells, strengthens the immune system and stimulates detoxification. It softens sudden painful inflammations. It accelerates the healing of sunburn and sunstroke. Ideal in the prophylaxis of allergies, reduces skin rashes as well as itching and flaking.

EFFECT ON PSYCHE

Overactive people become calmer and more balanced, calmer people get more energy for life. Fuchsite takes away anxiety and helps with depression and melancholy. It represents cheerfulness and a zest for life. In case of an inferiority complex, it builds a new self-confidence and in cases of stress, it strengthens serenity. It stimulates creativity, and keeps you mentally and physically agile.

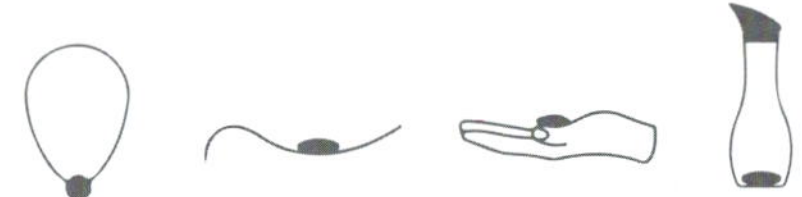

AQUARIS

GARNET

CONFIDENCE

HOPE

TRUST

SIGNIFICANCE

Garnet often occurs in magmatic stones, it generally belongs to the mineral class of insular silicates. It gives confidence and grip, gives hope and confidence in dealing with people, stimulates creativity. Since ancient times, it has been a guardian of true friendship. Brings joy and vitality; gives self-confidence, courage, energy, willpower.

EFFECT ON THE BODY

Garnet strengthens the heart muscle, stabilizes the blood circulation, helps against circulatory disorders, stimulates the production of red blood cells, improves the body's self-healing abilities. It regulates and strengthens the entire blood circulation, prevents anemia by increasing plasma and leukocytes, and stimulates blood circulation. In addition, it increases sexual power and resolves impotence.

EFFECT ON PSYCHE

Garnet brings joy and vitality; gives self-confidence, courage, energy, willpower and success. It helps against melancholy and depression. Garnet is one of the oldest healing crystals in the world, and its effects are well documented in all cultures. It is a stone that can improve dealing with taboo subjects, energetic blockages, painful experiences and embarrassment.

HALITE

MOOD-LIFTING
DYNAMIC
BALANCE

SIGNIFICANCE

Halite is a stone-forming mineral from the mineral class of halides. Halite protects against outside influences, makes one more aware of one's own events and helps to break away from entrenched patterns of thought and behavior. It gives more dynamics. Halite has a mood-lifting effect.

EFFECT ON THE BODY

Halite provides a well balanced electrolyte balance and ensures good fluid absorption. Thereby it strengthens the function of internal organs and beautifies the external appearance. The body becomes more active and feels a desire to move. When applied to painful areas, it gives relief. Therefore, sometimes the stone is used even after a long period of illness. It helps people get back on their feet again.

EFFECT ON PSYCHE

Halite helps against lack of drive and supports to develop a strong self-awareness. It stimulates the flow of personal energies. It stimulates the senses to deal with one's own behavioral habits as well as with the environment. Halite encourages the mind to engage in new ideas and spontaneous adventures. It can be used to act dynamically in important competitive situations.

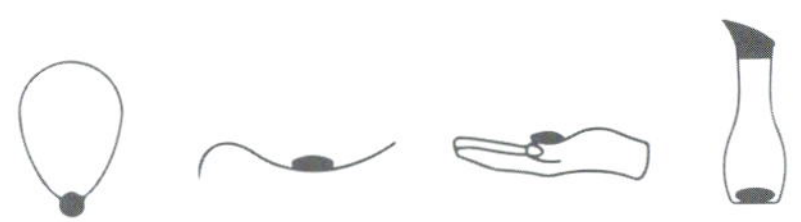

HOWLITE

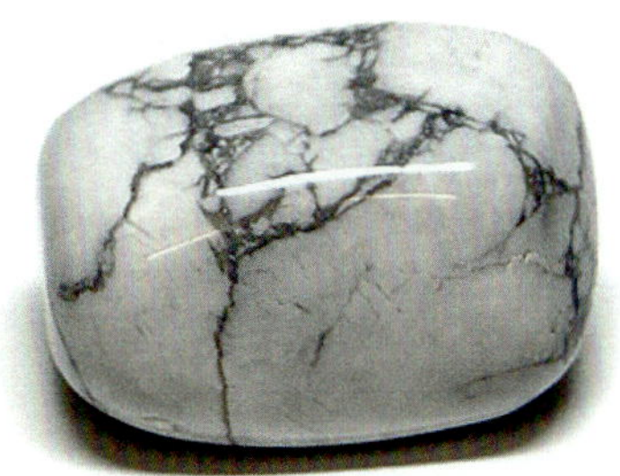

BETTER LIFE DESIGN
OPEN-MINDEDNESS

SIGNIFICANCE

Howlite is formed by the combination of boric acid and silicon dioxide, it belongs to the mineral class of silicates. Howlite encourages a better way of life, removes blockages and allows us to cope with new life situations. In addition, it can help make you more open-minded and give you more charisma.

EFFECT ON THE BODY

Howlite balances calcium in the body, relieves the effects of poisoning, stimulates regurgitation in nausea, good for chemical burns and contact poisoning. It has a dehydrating effect on the body, stimulates metabolism and eliminates combustion residues. It can also relieve frequent belching and heartburn, as well as gastritis caused by hyperacidity. Thanks to its high calcium content, it also has a positive effect on bones, joints, nails and teeth.

EFFECT ON PSYCHE

Strengthens the ability to judge and improves memory, reduces stress and feelings of anger, makes one steadfast and able to defend against unfair opponents. It calms people who are prone to outbursts of anger and temper. It neutralizes negative energies. Helps to more easily accept new life situations and especially to meet our fellow man with more open-mindedness and charm.

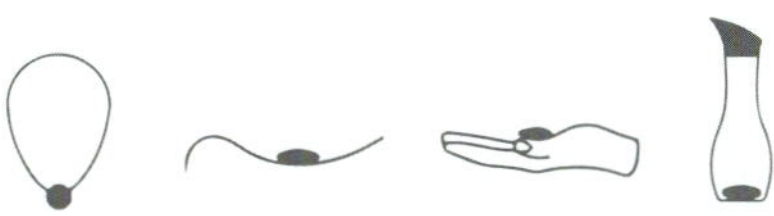

JADE

PROSPERITY
ABUNDANCE
SELF-REFLECTION

SIGNIFICANCE

Jade forms under extreme pressure and high temperatures and belongs to the mineral class of silicates. Jade opens the heart to all the wisdom, prosperity and unlimited possibilities that the universe offers. Jade guides the mind to a clear understanding of the greater plan.

EFFECT ON THE BODY

Jade stimulates kidney activity and the nervous system, detoxifies the organism, has a hemostatic effect, and strengthens the heart and blood circulation. Jade has very gentle vibrations that penetrate very deeply due to its high frequency. It has a beneficial effect on diseases of the internal organs and intestinal tract. It strengthens the entire immune system, in addition, jade supports the expulsion of toxins.

EFFECT ON PSYCHE

Jade has a balancing effect on all the senses. Helps in self-knowledge and self-realization. The balance and inner peace that you get from jade ensures that this stone also stimulates love. It gives you a zest for life, joy and open-mindedness. Helps you to disconnect, become calmer and reflect.

CANCER   LIBRA

JASPER

STABILITY
SUPPORT
ACTIVITY

SIGNIFICANCE

Jasper is a fine-grained quartz. It assists in strengthening one's foundation, provides stability in life to act successfully. Helps to take on new tasks, manage conflicts and seek creative solutions.

EFFECT ON THE BODY

Red Jasper stops bleeding, stimulates circulation and energy flow, relieves bloating, flatulence and nausea. Is helpful in diseases of the gall bladder, kidneys and liver. Good for stomach, intestines, liver, pregnancy, childbirth, sexual organs. Furthermore, in women it stimulates a regular menstrual cycle and activates the reproductive organs of both sexes. Jasper water before meals cures stomach diseases.

EFFECT ON PSYCHE

This stone can be comforting. Red Jasper awakens and activates all areas of the body that feel sluggish or inactive. It strengthens self-confidence, willpower and perseverance. It is a stone for vitality and dynamism and stimulates the readiness to deal with conflicts, relieves nervousness, jumpiness, stress. It gives inner contentment and acts against inner restlessness, but also against lack of will, aimlessness.

JET

NEW BEGINNINGS
COURAGE
RELIEF

SIGNIFICANCE

Jet was formed in swampy areas and is bitumen-rich brown coal. Agate is considered a protective stone against grief. According to tradition, Jet gives you courage, helps to cope with grief or sorrow and thus paves the way for a new beginning. In addition, it prevents you from bad thoughts and helps with depression.

EFFECT ON THE BODY

It has strong effects on the respiratory system and also protects joints and bones from wear and inflammation. The Jet also helps with tooth and jaw pain. One has a positive experience when using to treat tinitus.

EFFECT ON PSYCHE

It makes it easier to make a fresh start. When the soul suffers from the loss of a loved one or animal, it gives us renewed courage to live. It saves you from rash actions and suicide. This stone brings light and warmth, awakening in the soul the desire to live. Tolerance and understanding are further virtues to come back to the center and to encounter life in a new way. A stone for character training, it helps to jump over one's own shadow. It brings about discipline and responsibility towards one's neighbor.

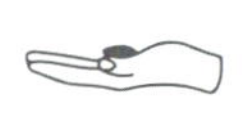
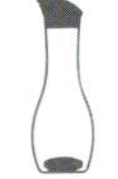

KUNZITE

LOVE
COMFORT
TRUST

SIGNIFICANCE

Kunzite, like hiddenite and triphan, is a variety of the mineral spodumene. It belongs to the mineral class of silicates. Kunzite is a calming crystal that connects heart and head, aligning emotional and mental aspects. Strengthens trust in people where relationships are torturous, helps to open up to love and regain a sense of trust and hope.

EFFECT ON THE BODY

Kunzite strengthens and supports the heart muscles, stimulates the production of hormones, relieves back pain, helps with nervous disorders. It controls the function of white and red blood cells and ensures better oxygen absorption. Reduces high blood pressure.

EFFECT ON PSYCHE

Kunzite brings inner peace, vitality, love and gives more devotion. It increases empathy, improves contact with the environment and helps to handle criticism better. It also reduces inhibitions and feelings of inferiority and encourages people to step over their own shadow. In case of inner turmoil, worries, fears or depression, Kunzite is a good aid, because it brightens up the mood again.

LABRADORITE

LIMITLESS POTENTIAL
CONSCIOUSNESS

SIGNIFICANCE

Labradorite is assigned to the feldspar group, it belongs to the mineral class of silicates. Labradorite helps to reach a higher state of consciousness and strengthens mental and spiritual power. Supports oneself in finding your true goals.

EFFECT ON THE BODY

Labradorite helps with digestive, circulatory, and metabolic problems, and with poor eyesight. Relieves sensitivity to cold, rheumatism and gout, stabilizes the acid-base balance of the body, has a blood pressure lowering effect. Stimulates self-healing powers, activates muscles, helps against circulatory problems and eye problems. This stone strengthens the immune system and the thymus gland.

EFFECT ON PSYCHE

Labradorite inspires the imagination with its variety of colors, increases creativity and improves memory. It also strengthens intuition and promotes a rational sense of reality. Labradorite helps to intensify one's feelings, illustrating one's intentions. Due to its calming and balancing effect, labradorite helps with a quick-tempered mood.

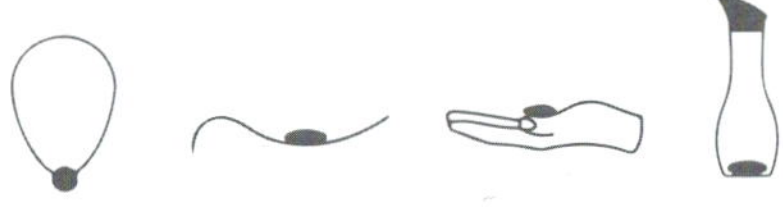

CANCER

LAPIS LAZULI

AWARENESS
INNER WISDOM
TRUST

SIGNIFICANCE

Lapis lazuli is a mineral mixture that was formed mainly by the transformation of lime to marble. It belongs to the mineral class of silicates. The stone helps to get rid of bad Habits and stimulates the ability to criticize. In addition, it creates new self-confidence and makes it easier to get depressing burdens off one's chest. Lapis lazuli can stimulate a clear mind, concentration and intuition.

EFFECT ON THE BODY

Strengthens the functioning of various glands of the body, lowers blood pressure, and prevents skin diseases. Prevents plaque build-up in blood vessels, reducing strokes and heart attacks. Helps with skin rashes, insect bites, warts, pain and swelling, relieves headache, and strengthens eyesight.

EFFECT ON PSYCHE

Lapis lazuli is the stone of kings. Needs for friendship, love and partnership are encouraged. It helps to reduce fears and prejudices. Lapis lazuli makes us cultivate friendships and partnerships more intimately. It has a very intuitive, invigorating and concentration-enhancing effect and gives more ingenuity and thinking ability.

LARIMAR

NEW HORIZONS
DISSOLVING OLD PATTERNS
INNER PEACE

SIGNIFICANCE

Larimar forms hydrothermally in basalt, it belongs to the mineral class of silicates. The sky-blue Larimar expands the mental horizon and enables new ways of seeing. In this way, this healing crystal helps to dissolve limiting thought patterns and reshape life. Larimar gives inner peace and is a protective stone used against negative energies.

EFFECT ON THE BODY

Larimar stimulates self-healing, boosts brain activity. It is a skeletal stone that has a positive effect on bone structure and joints. Acts against stiffness of muscles, tendons and joints. Its healing functi-on is especially effective on the limbs such as hands, feet, legs, etc. It can relieve sciatic pain and lumbago.

EFFECT ON PSYCHE

Larimar is also called "Atlantis stone". It promotes good sleep and beautiful dreams, embodies peace and clarity, radiates healing and loving energies, brings inner peace, and promotes mental and physical growth. Helps against anxiety, blockages and depression. Its appearance conveys freshness and liveliness, thus it has a posi-tive effect on depression and the search for new perspectives. It is helpful in times of change, stimulates our inspiration and self-realization.

LEO

LEMON CALCITE

MENTAL DEVELOPMENT
STRONG MEMORY

SIGNIFICANCE

Calcite is a stone-forming mineral, it belongs as calcium carbonate to the mineral class of carbonates. Lemon calcite brings us more zest for life and increases self-confidence. Thanks to its help, memory and thinking skills are strengthened, giving more steadfastness and drive in problematic situations.

EFFECT ON THE BODY

Lemon calcite stimulates metabolism, promotes cell growth and strengthens the immune system. Improves blood coagulation. Constricted coronary arteries, low blood pressure, cardiac arrhythmias and heart attacks are positively influenced by lemon calcite. Helps with bone diseases, fractures, gout, rheumatism, osteoarthritis, arthritis, and osteoporosis.

EFFECT ON PSYCHE

Lemon calcite is a "hope stone" that gives us cordiality, charity and cheerfulness. It accelerates one's mental development, strengthens drive and memory. It gives self-confidence and steadfastness. Its radiant color has a mood-lifting effect.

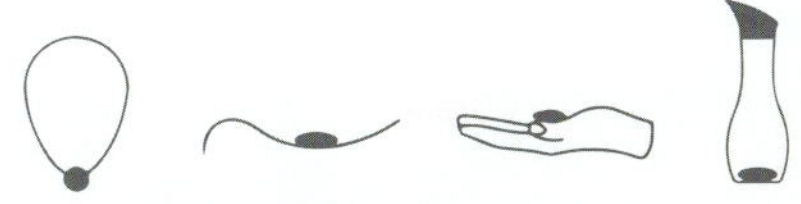

LEOPARD JASPER

SELF-HEALING

GROUNDING

PROTECTION

SIGNIFICANCE

Leopard jasper is a fine-grained quartz. It improves stamina and strengthens the bladder. It is intended to contribute to self-healing and spiritual growth. Jasper is a very stable, grounding and protective stone.

EFFECT ON THE BODY

This jasper has a strong draining and cleansing effect on the liver, gall bladder, kidneys and bladder. It also has a soothing effect on severe stomach and abdominal pain and prevents hiccups, nausea and hyperthyroidism. It is also recommended for painful hardening of muscle tissues, especially for neck, shoulder, back and buttock muscles, it has a relaxing effect.

EFFECT ON PSYCHE

Leopard jasper gives stamina, inspires the imagination and has a calming effect on the soul. It soothes relationship anxiety or jealousy. It also strengthens the connection with nature and empathy for animals. Leopard jasper traditionally helps to connect with animals. It is a very strong self-healing and nurturing stone that helps to boost personal growth. It calms in stressful times and stimulates inner peace.

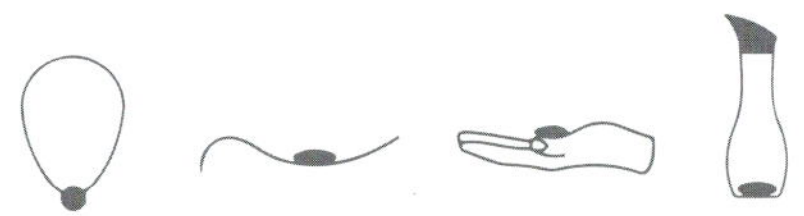

"""

LEPIDOLITE

INNER PEACE
BALANCE

SIGNIFICANCE

Lepidolite belongs as mica to the mineral class of silicates. As a protective stone, it gives inner peace, stimulates self-determination and self-discipline. Furthermore, the lepidolite strengthens the senses and makes you, depending on the temperament, calmer and more balanced, but also more outgoing.

EFFECT ON THE BODY

Lepidolite promotes digestion, firms the skin, stabilizes the blood circulation, has a detoxifying effect, helps with hyperacidity and stimulates the cleansing process of the skin and connective tissue. It supports the liver, protects against infections, strengthens the joints and is very popular as a therapeutic crystal after suffering a stroke.

EFFECT ON PSYCHE

Lepidolite relieves stress and depression, has a refreshing effect, promotes self-love and tolerance. It strengthens openness and sincerity. Has a calming effect, stimulates independence and self-discipline. It brings you joy, tranquility, inner peace and decisiveness. Lepidolite - the stone to completely disconnect, relieve the nerves and give yourself peace of mind.

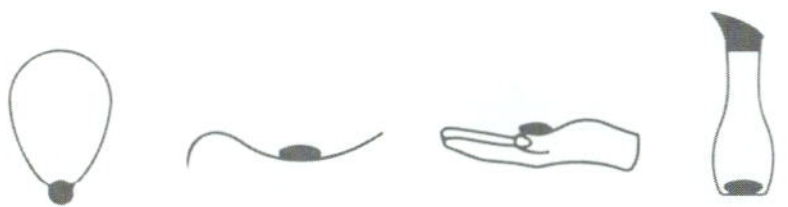

MAGNESITE

RELAXATION
OPTIMISM
SELF-DETERMINATION

SIGNIFICANCE

Magnesite is formed mainly during the weathering of magnesium-bearing stones; it belongs to the mineral class of carbonates. Magnesite is very good for balance and relaxation. In this way, it contributes to self-determination. However, this healing crystal also stimulates patience as well as sympathy and the quality of having an open ear for other people.

EFFECT ON THE BODY

Magnesite contributes to cell purification, strengthens and calms the heart, helps with fever and chills, has a detoxifying and anti-spasmodic effect. Helps with biliousness, migraines, headaches and cramps of internal organs, inhibits blood clotting, reduces thrombosis, stimulates the breakdown of fatty deposits in the vessels and thus helps prevent heart attacks. Supports the lowering of cholesterol levels. Helps you to lose weight and excessive body odor. It cleanses cells, kidneys, bile and bladder from deposits and stones.

EFFECT ON PSYCHE

Magnesite brings inner peace, instills serenity and relaxation. Acts against nervousness, irritability, anger, helps with depression, nervous tension, excitability, anxiety and hypersensitivity. Provides balance and strengthens the ability to express oneself. In meditation, magnesite brings inner peace and stimulates the imagination.

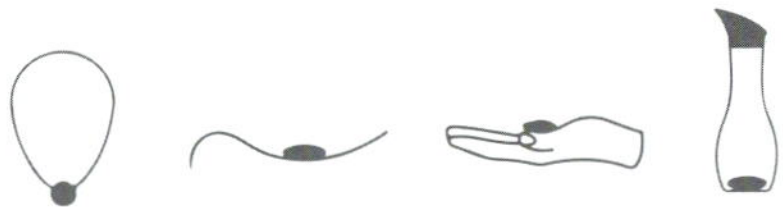

MAGNETITE

CLARITY
HIGHER GOALS
FLEXIBILITY

SIGNIFICANCE

Magnetite is a ferromagnetic mineral, it belongs to the mineral class of oxides. Magnetite helps to separate the important from the unimportant and to set clear priorities. It also mitigates sticking to outdated values and can increase responsiveness.

EFFECT ON THE BODY

Magnetite balances the feeling of hunger and thirst, regulates blood sugar levels and purifies the blood, strengthens the pancreas, relieves cramps, strengthens the circulation, helps with pneumonia and liver problems. Thanks to its magnetic properties, it has a harmonizing effect on the hypothalamus, helps renew cells and accelerates the purification of the organism.

EFFECT ON PSYCHE

Magnetite gives vitality, willpower and the ability to immediately turn decisions into actions. It helps to distinguish what is good for you and what is not. It brings warmth and thus also provides relaxation in the mental sphere, helps to release internal blockages, provides mental balance and relaxation. It is balancing, connecting and strengthening the nerves. Magnetite enables us to let go of mental baggage and thus live more lighthearted, happier and more carefree.

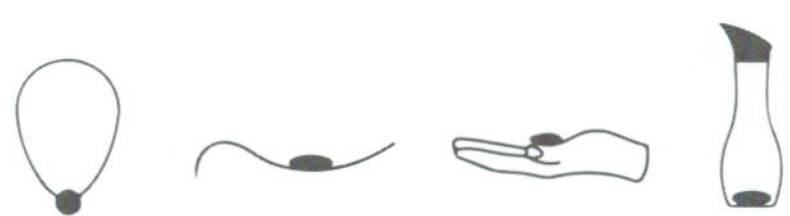

MALACHITE

TRANSFORMATION
CHANGE
REFLECTION

SIGNIFICANCE

Malachite is a copper carbonate, it belongs to the mineral class of carbonates. Malachite is what you ask when you want unfiltered advice regarding your finances and love life. Its energy helps you to think about changing certain aspects of your life to change negative patterns.

EFFECT ON THE BODY

Malachite helps with diseases of the bones and spine, for example, disc problems, rheumatism and joint inflammation, has a decramping effect, strengthens the heart muscle, stabilizes and strengthens the cardiovascular system. Relieves severe menstrual pain and assists in childbirth, hence its popular name "midwife stone". It activates self-healing powers, brings you relief for sprains and bruises.

EFFECT ON PSYCHE

Malachite inspires the imagination, improves perception and increases concentration. It also brings more understanding and love for the environment. With more balance, malachite raises the quality of life and also contributes to a more harmonious partnership. In addition, malachite helps to make the right decisions. Malachite is also a comforting companion due to a heartbreak.

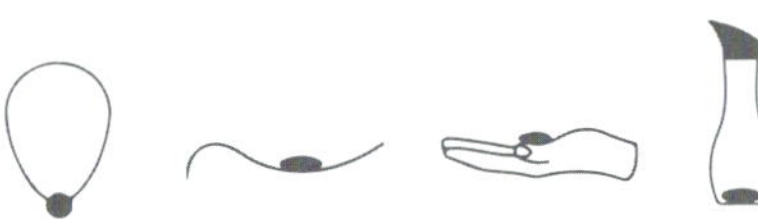

MILK OPAL

ACCEPTANCE
POSITIVE FEELINGS
JOY OF LIFE

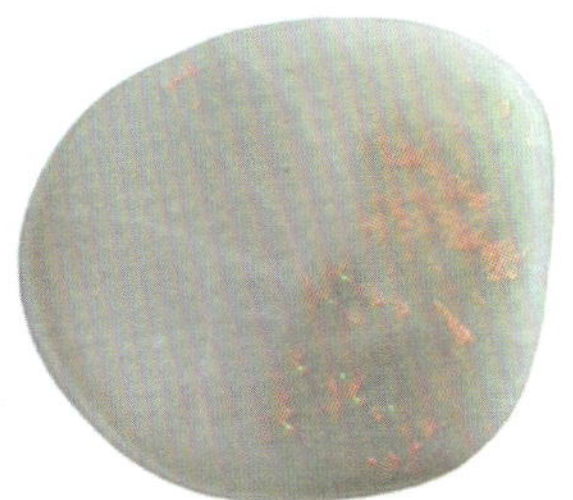

SIGNIFICANCE

Milk opal is formed by the desiccation of hydrous silica, it belongs to the mineral class of oxides. Opals have always been considered soothing to the soul, as just looking at them brings inner joy. They promote qualities such as acceptance, a sense of community and communication skills.

EFFECT ON THE BODY

Milk opal supports the stomach and intestines and strengthens the heart. It helps against digestive problems, also for the treatment of eating disorders such as anorexia, the healing crystal is sometimes used. In addition, it can act against anemia and relieve rheumatic complaints. Helpful for people who are going through puberty and are going through a major physical and psychological change.

EFFECT ON PSYCHE

The opal awakens the joy of life in people. The healing crystal provides the right amount of serenity and at the same time instigates creative achievements. In some cases, it eliminates inner aimlessness and liberates people from personal inertia. The healing crystal is also successfully used against burnout.

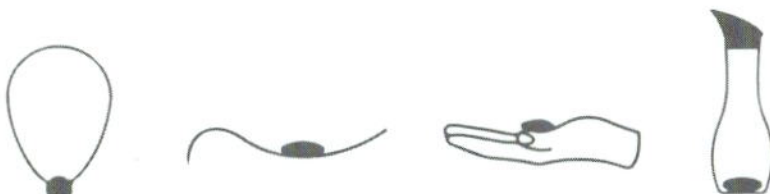

MOLDAVITE

CHEERFULNESS
SPIRITUAL OPENNESS
EMPATHY

SIGNIFICANCE

Moldavite consists of up to 80 percent silicon dioxide, it belongs to the mineral class of oxides. Moldavite gives vitality, cheerfulness and opens the mind. Thus, this healing crystal increases resourcefulness and helps to find solutions to problems. Balances out aggression.

EFFECT ON THE BODY

Moldavite supports healing processes in almost all infectious diseases. It protects the blood from diseases by strengthening the white blood cells, which are responsible for defending against infections and destroying bacteria. Moldavite binds iron and protects bone marrow, which is responsible for the formation of white blood cells.

EFFECT ON PSYCHE

Moldavite stimulates sensitivity and lets us consciously experience the noble things in life. We receive signals on how we can achieve more positive things with our spiritual powers. Moldavite is one of the most important intuition stones. It inspires the imagination, gives spontaneous ideas and stimulates creativity. It gives us more conscious life energy, joy and harmonizes the partnership.

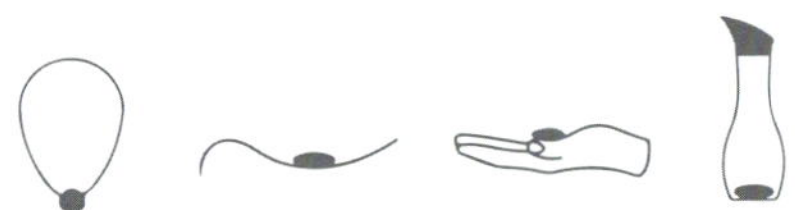

MOOKAITE

BALANCE
DETERMINATION
FLEXIBILITY

SIGNIFICANCE

Mookaite is formed from silicon dioxide, it belongs to the mineral class of oxides. It is said that Mookaite combines the properties of yellow and red jasper and thus gives us more peace and balance. It helps to implement ideas or goals with dynamism and enthusiasm. It brings mental flexibility and expands the mental horizon.

EFFECT ON THE BODY

To this day, Mookaite is valued as a strong healing crystal. It acts against inflammations. Physically, it gives a healthy vitality and supports blood purification and the entire immune system. Mookaite helps with infections of all kinds and can also be used to help with eczema, suppurated injuries, pimples and acne, and even insect bites. It strengthens the power and vitality of the whole body.

EFFECT ON PSYCHE

Mookaite stands for inner balance, activity, creativity, vitality, adventurousness. You could even call it a lucky stone. It levels the polarity between serenity and drive, relaxation and recreation. It helps to get fully involved: with the people and the landscape. It opens the soul to fine sensations and sensual enrichment. Mookaite loves freedom, but values friendship even more.

MOONSTONE

LIFE PURPOSE
NEW BEGINNINGS
DESTINY

SIGNIFICANCE

Moonstone is a variety of orthoclase and belongs to the feldspar group. It is assigned to the mineral class of silicates. It supports the realization of wishes and dreams. It also helps to increase fertility.

EFFECT ON THE BODY

It has a particularly intense effect on the female reproductive organs, regulates hormonal balance, thereby promoting fertility and helps with menstrual cramps. It alleviates pregnancy discomfort, helps with involution, has a regulating effect on milk production and is a good companion during menopause.

EFFECT ON PSYCHE

Moonstone, as the name suggests, can protect against moon addiction. To do this, it should be placed under your pillow for a whole moon phase. Furthermore, it strengthens intuition and intensifies feelings. It activates empathy and stimulates love. Moonstone works especially well for women. It gives them vitality, cheerfulness as well as balance and gives a youthful appearance. Moonstone is also capable of alleviating anxiety.

MORGANITE (BERYL)

RESPONSIBILITY
CALMNESS

SIGNIFICANCE

Manganite is formed magmatically or hydrothermally, it belongs to the mineral class of silicates. Manganite provides relaxation, peace, serenity and gives us confidence. It relieves anxiety, pressure to perform as well as stress and helps to overcome bad times and face unpleasant situations.

EFFECT ON THE BODY

Manganite stimulates the liver and thus ensures a good detoxification of the body. Helpful for travel constipation or diarrhea, acts on angina, bronchitis, eye ailments and stress. White beryl is a very gentle healing crystal. It helps with stomach and intestinal inflammation and hemorrhoids.

EFFECT ON PSYCHE

Morganite awakens personal energies and provides a positive aura. Helps us to feel more comfortable in a new life situation. Strengthens in cases of mental restlessness, makes us calmer, serene and more self-confident.

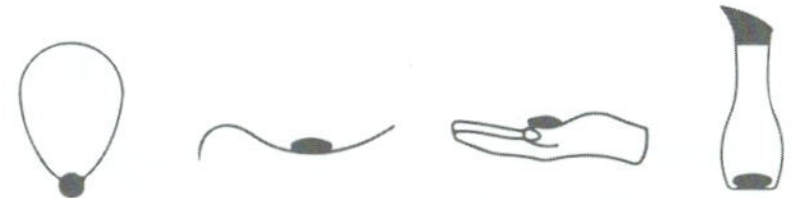

MOSS AGATE

STRONG AWARENESS
COMMUNICATION

SIGNIFICANCE

It forms from silicon dioxide and belongs to the mineral class of oxides. Moss agate dissolves old patterns, increases consciousness, frees you from old burdens and helps to develop strategies for a successful future. It increases self-awareness and the ability to communicate, and above all helps to regain courage in difficult situations and to approach problems optimistically.

EFFECT ON THE BODY

Moss agate helps against fungi and viruses, has a strengthening effect on the pancreas and stimulates insulin production. Strengthens the filtering organs such as kidneys, spleen and liver. The water balance is better regulated in the whole organism. Protects against infestation of viruses, fungi, etc. Stimulates all sebaceous glands, so it gives the skin and hair more suppleness and a healthier appearance.

EFFECT ON PSYCHE

Moss agate represents confidence, creativity, recreation, love of nature, better perception of the environment. It helps against anxiety and strengthens interest in all important things in life. The stone helps to keep the overview and opens the eyes for a success-ful life design. Increases general well-being and strengthens self-confidence.

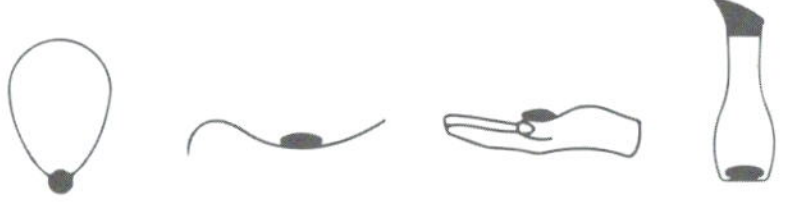

CAPRICORNUS

NEPHRITE (JADE)

RIGHT DECISIONS
INNER PEACE

SIGNIFICANCE

Nephrite is formed during the stone metamorphism of serpentine and actinolite, it belongs to the mineral class of silicates. Nephrite is a stone for the longing for happiness. In addition, it helps to preserve one's identity in difficult times. It reduces tension or worry. Stimulates balance and inner peace and helps to make the right decisions.

EFFECT ON THE BODY

Nephrite deacidifies and drains, supports body detoxification and strengthens kidneys, bladder and liver. It is effective against gout and kidney stones. It acts especially on the heart and thymus gland. It prevents seizures and kidney congestion during pregnancy. Strengthens the immune system, stimulates metabolism and fights infections, jaundice and fever.

EFFECT ON PSYCHE

Nephrite cools overheated tempers, gives gentleness without tendency to give in. Stands for peace, harmony and creativity. Acts against hectic times and restlessness. It brings joy from the depths of the soul, conveys peaceful feelings, harmony, balance and serenity. Nephrite strengthens courage and expressiveness, at the same time it stimulates the ability to love.

OBSIDIAN

SELF REFLECTION
PROTECTION
PURIFICATION

SIGNIFICANCE

Obsidian or volcanic glass is formed by rapidly cooled lava droplets. It does not count as a mineral, but is assigned to the class of stones. Black obsidian is particularly good at dissolving blockages, shock, anxiety and trauma. It also alleviates associated pain from past experiences. It also promotes unused skills and improves perception.

EFFECT ON THE BODY

Obsidian is a wound healing crystal. Especially cuts especially close faster. Connective tissue, blood, skin and bones benefit in particular from its action. It has a calming and stabilizing effect on the stomach and intestines and reduces asthma symptoms. Vitamin C can be better absorbed. Obsidian helps with circulatory problems, pain, tension and muscle spasms. Furthermore, it strengthens the spine, skin and hair.

EFFECT ON PSYCHE

It's hard to confront the bad and ugly parts of ourselves, but Obsidian makes it easier. It shows a reflection of the true self and helps to accept oneself completely. Harsh realities are made more bearable by Obsidian. It provides a complete overview of oneself, including all positive and negative qualities.

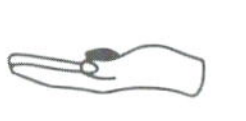

SCORPIUS   SAGITTARIUS

OCEAN AGATE
CHALCEDONY

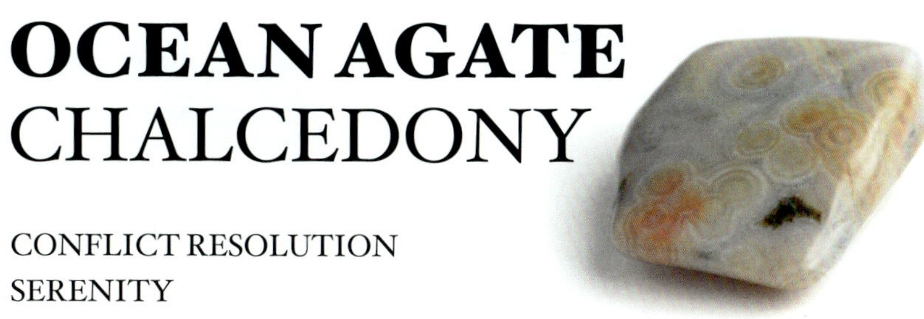

CONFLICT RESOLUTION
SERENITY

SIGNIFICANCE

Ocean agate is a mixture of chalcedony and jasper, it belongs to the mineral class of oxides. This stone helps to resolve conflicts. In addition, it gives serenity, makes you feel confident and ensures a pleasant sleep. Stimulates spiritual renewal, sparks the imagination, brings liveliness. It gives a positive attitude to life and increases resilience.

EFFECT ON THE BODY

Ocean agate is said to have a rejuvenating effect. It stimulates the blood circulation and strengthens the functions of the organs. In addition, it works very well to stabilize the immune system. Indigestion, nausea and bloating are other physical ailments that ocean agate effectively relieves.

EFFECT ON PSYCHE

Ocean agate strengthens self-confidence, willpower and stamina. It is a stone for vitality and dynamism, stimulates the readiness for conflict, helps against nervousness, jumpiness, stress and recklessness. It gives one inner satisfaction and acts against inner restlessness, but also against aimlessness. Boosts steadfastness, strengthens willpower and assertiveness.

ONYX

ZEST FOR LIFE
SELF-CONFIDENCE
RESISTANCE

SIGNIFICANCE

Onyx, as a variety of chalcedony, belongs to the quartz and to the mineral class of oxides. The onyx is a particularly strong stone to increase self-confidence and resilience. Thus, the onyx brings more zest for life. Also, it gives life more stability and activates the perseverance.

EFFECT ON THE BODY

Black onyx strengthens blood circulation and boosts the immune system. Onyx improves the sense of hearing and heals diseases of the inner ear, in some cases also relieves ringing in the ears or helps with hearing loss. Also disorders effecting one's sense of balance are improved by onyx. In general, it promotes the function of motor and sensory nerves and thus also helps with visual impairment. Like all chalcedony, it strengthens the immune system.

EFFECT ON PSYCHE

Onyx stands for self-confidence and perseverance. The onyx establishes greater harmony between our outer shell and core, giving more resilience, stability and vitality. Onyx first strengthens the ego, it gives firmness and constancy to bitterness. . It perfectly strengthens concentration. Especially for people who are easily influenced, it helps to develop a healthy ego and to keep an eye on one's own ideas and perceptions.

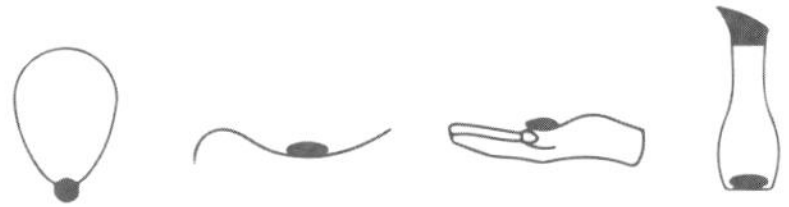

CAPRICORNUS

OPAL

HAPPINESS
ACCEPTANCE
DETERMINATION

SIGNIFICANCE

Opal is formed by the desiccation of hydrous silica. This stone belongs to the mineral class of oxides. It develops the greatest effect when observed, creates feelings of happiness by activating our inner harmony. It thus increases the belief in oneself as well as the will for self-realization.

EFFECT ON THE BODY

Opals strengthen the digestive system and support all corresponding organs. Opal is a healthy blood builder, all parts in the blood are supported more intensively. It promotes oxygen absorption and the transport of all vital nutrients. Improves the metabolism of the subcutaneous tissue and helps to better store collagens, resulting in a better, smoother skin appearance.

EFFECT ON PSYCHE

Opal stands for joy, love of life, serenity, creativity and helps against inhibitions and depression. It is a gemstone that gives one joy and serenity through its play of colors. Awakens the childlike experience and stimulates the flow of energy in the body, removes blockages and depression. It raises the well-being. Goals and life desires are achieved very consistently with the help of opals.

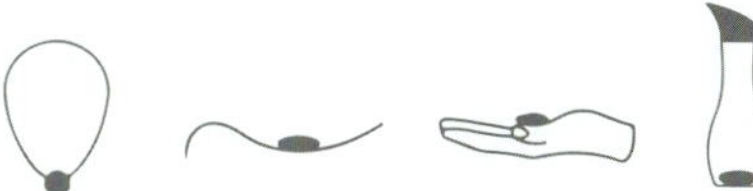

PERIDOT

POSITIVITY
INNER BALANCE

SIGNIFICANCE

Peridot belongs to the olivine group and forms in deeper basic igneous stones, it belongs to the mineral class of silicates. The peridot is able to turn negative feelings such as selfishness, envy or heartlessness into positive feelings . In this way, it not only improves the relationship with fellow human beings, but also reduces anger, pain or remorse.

EFFECT ON THE BODY

Peridot with a homeopathic approach causes excellent detoxification of the body, strengthens the liver, gall bladder and kidneys. Also helps with disorders of the skin such as acne, pimples and warts.

EFFECT ON PSYCHE

Peridot with its profound effects has a very positive influence on our inner balance. It gifts us a more positive outlook on life. Negative feelings such as envy, selfishness and coldness of feeling are transformed into a positive attitude towards life with the help of the peridot. On a psychological level, it addresses healing grief work and alleviates pent-up anger and rage as well as feelings of guilt and self-blame.

PETRIFIED WOOD

RELAXATION
MINDFULNESS

SIGNIFICANCE

Petrified wood forms during the petrification of fossil woods. It brings us rest, strengthens attention and helps to avoid being distracted again and again. In this context, it confers the ability to direct one's actions towards a specific goal and to complete what has been started.

EFFECT ON THE BODY

The petrified wood is a classic stone with regards to the subject of bones and joints. In any form of use, whether as a tumbled stone for laying on, as a gemstone or as crystal water, it immediately detects and combats disorders such as arthritis, arthritis or gout. Mouthwashes with crystal water from petrified wood are good for teeth - a very gentle way to help with root canal treatment.

EFFECT ON PSYCHE

Petrified wood penetrates us with all its colors and gives us more balance and a calmer way of life. It brings about an inner, calming lasting strength. Modesty, nature-loving sense of beauty, love of home, love of the familiar are other aspects. It can answer questions like, "Where is my place in life?" "How do I design my living space?" "How do I use my time in life?" Petrified wood provides one with energy as well as recreation.

PEARL

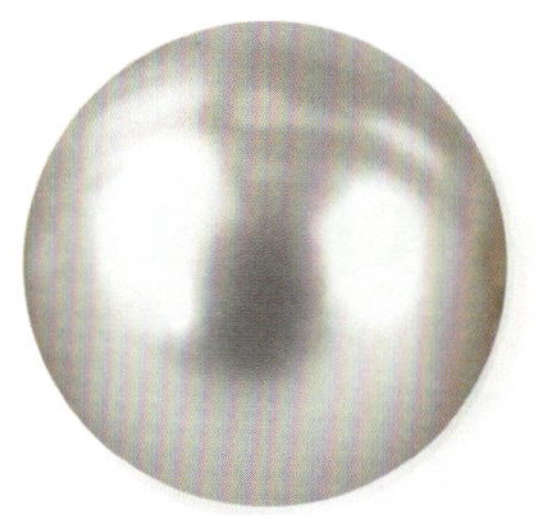

SPIRITUAL GROWTH
LIFE EXPERIENCE
PEACE OF MIND

SIGNIFICANCE

The inner shell layer of many marine mollusks is called mother-of-pearl, it is assigned to the mineral class of carbonates. Pearls contribute to the experience of life. They show the way to successfully deal with problems. One discovers blockages or traumas and finds a way to overcome them. They promote spiritual growth and give more peace of mind.

EFFECT ON THE BODY

The Chinese discovered the effect of this mineral from the sea many millennia ago. They used it as an aphrodisiac and used its energies against melancholic moods. Mother of pearl can be used to reawaken the life forces of men. It supports rehabilitation after periods of illness, while mother-of-pearl acts not only on the physical level.

EFFECT ON PSYCHE

The stone from the depths of the sea has a harmonizing and calming effect on the soul. Helps overcome inner conflicts to emerge stronger from crises. Some people use the glimmering material when they are plagued by mental turmoil or have trouble sleeping. Pearls strengthen the sense of beauty and nobility in life, while promoting their own excellence.

PYRITE

SELF-KNOWLEDGE
CONFIDENCE
UNBLOCKING

SIGNIFICANCE

Pyrite can be formed in many ways from an iron-sulfur compound; it belongs to the mineral class of sulfides. With pyrite you gain self-knowledge, because it makes you think about yourself. In this way, it reveals the possible cause of blockages and helps to solve them. Even persistent stress, nervousness or inner restlessness can be solved with the help of pyrite. It gives you a new confidence.

EFFECT ON THE BODY

Pyrite strengthens the nerves and has a positive effect on the physical condition. It dulls certain pains and is therefore used as a healing crystal for sciatic pain and arthritis. Pyrite can positively influence digestion. Thus, the stone creates a good physical well-being.

EFFECT ON PSYCHE

The pyrite has a very conductive and purifying function on the mind due to its metallic properties. It dissolves blockages and frees from fears such as exam anxiety and contact inhibitions. We are quicker to recognize dead ends in our lives and receive new hope that makes life more worth living. It enables to distinguish good from evil and helps to avoid disagreements, it also strengthens one's inner fire.

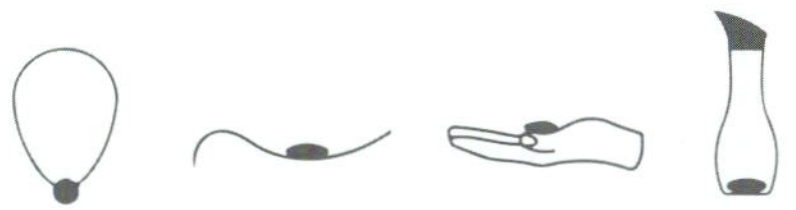

RAINBOW OBSIDIAN

SPIRITUAL POWER
RECOGNITION

SIGNIFICANCE

Obsidian or volcanic glass is formed by rapidly cooled lava droplets. It does not count as a mineral, but is assigned to the class of stones. Rainbow obsidian provides protection, improves mental strength and strengthens perception. It gives the ability to recognize one's own weaknesses and supports the therapy for addictions.

EFFECT ON THE BODY

Rainbow obsidian harmonizes the function of the glands and ensures adequate hormone production, as it strengthens the thyroid, ovaries, pancreas, adrenal gland and pituitary gland. It coordinates the cerebral hemispheres with each other and supports the control of the nervous system.

EFFECT ON PSYCHE

Rainbow obsidian helps to bring hidden things from the subconscious into consciousness. In doing so, blockages, fears and states of shock are released. It grounds the individual and thus establishes a connection to essential life. As a protective stone, it stabilizes energies and protects from physical as well as emotional harm.

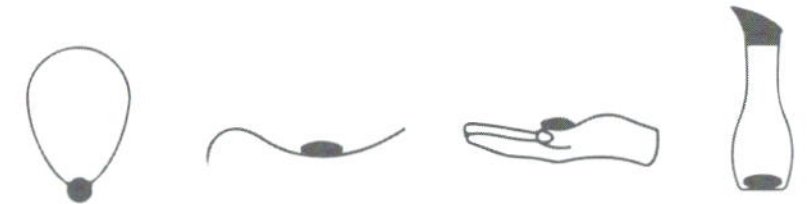

RHODOCHROSITE

ALIGNMENT
BALANCE
OPENNESS

SIGNIFICANCE

Rhodochrosite forms predominantly secondarily in the oxidation zone (the zone between the earth's surface and the groundwater level), where carbonated water combines with manganese oxide. It belongs to the mineral class of carbonates. Rhodochrosite promotes self-knowledge and helps in a possible transformation of life. It lets you see new perspectives and gain more zest for life.

EFFECT ON THE BODY

Rhodochrosite strengthens the pancreas and spleen, alleviates digestive problems, liver disorders, respiratory and lung diseases. It is beneficial in diabetes and kidney disease. Eliminates skin impurities, acne and pimples. It strengthens the heart and eyesight.

EFFECT ON PSYCHE

Rhodochrosite activates the whole body feeling with the help of its gentle waves and gives more contentment and honest love. Placed under your pillow, this stone will protect you from anxiety, existential fear and nightmares. It is the flirt stone in the flesh. It awakens sensuality and really piques your interest in the opposite sex . It produces a surplus of energy and makes you daring, hungry for experience, outgoing, spontaneous and high-spirited, according to the motto: "Cheeky goes a long way."

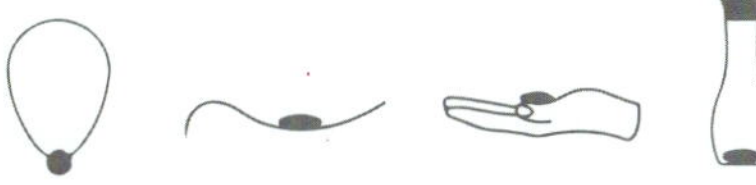

RHODONITE

INNER PEACE
HIGH RESILIENCE
UNDERSTANDING

SIGNIFICANCE

Rhodonite is formed mainly during the metamorphism of manganiferous stones, it belongs to the mineral class of silicates. Rhodonite helps to deal with any kind of life changes and to enter a new stage with more optimism. In conflicts, it provides more understanding and thus contributes to a better solution.

EFFECT ON THE BODY

Rhodonite is a very comprehensive healing crystal. It especially strengthens the heart and blood circulation and supports the strengthening and healing of the respiratory tract. As a typical first aid stone, it is of course also suitable for the care of wounds of all kinds. It promotes an improvement in the skin's appearance and has a very positive effect on scar healing. The pain-relieving manganese strengthens the body's own defenses.

EFFECT ON PSYCHE

It brings us more joy and confidence for coming changes and helps to be more open to a higher self-realization. Especially for exams and new tasks, the rhodonite protects against exam anxiety and learning blockades. These powers of rhodonite are especially helpful for teenagers and children. It helps to react calmly in dangerous situations and to keep your nerves. It can help you to cope with shocks and horrors while being mentally fit on.

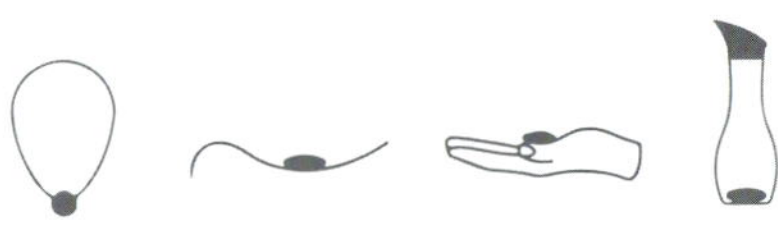

ROSE QUARTZ

FEARLESSNESS
TRUST IN YOURSELF

SIGNIFICANCE

Rose quartz is a pink-colored variety of quartz from the mineral class of oxides. It is a particularly important healing crystal for the heart. It ensures that relationship fears and anxieties in dealing with other people disappear. It prevents the inner closure, helps you to let go. In this way, the gemstone can also heal spiritual wounds.

EFFECT ON THE BODY

Rose quartz is the heart stone not only emotionally, but also physically. Rose quartz harmonizes the heart rhythm and strengthens the heart. It stimulates tissue circulation and thus the supply of nutrients in the cells. At the same time, it is said to help with blood diseases. For women, it has a fertility-enhancing effect.

EFFECT ON PSYCHE

Rose quartz can be a new foundation stone for a pure and unprejudiced new beginning in a partnership. It has a very invigorating power on both our creative thoughts and our imagination. It helps to stand by one's feelings and to develop according to one's own predispositions. Rose quartz makes one receptive to the beauty in life, for pleasure and sensuality. It increases empathy, soothes the mind and strengthens one's needs and the urge to fulfill them.

  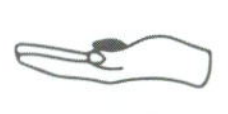   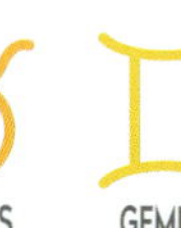   

RUBY

SELF-REALIZATION
DEVOTION
DETERMINATION

SIGNIFICANCE

Ruby is a red variety of corundum, it belongs to the mineral class of oxides. Ruby is one of the strongest gemstones for partnership, love and sexuality. Sexual dysfunction can be resolved by the ruby. It gifts us with vitality and devotion, but also morality and determination. It brings us closer to self-realization.

EFFECT ON THE BODY

Ruby helps with viral diseases, epidemics, fever, gout, diseases of the heart and blood circulation. It regulates low blood pressure. Ruby strengthens eyesight and helps with menstrual cramps. It stimulates metabolism, strengthens the nerves and the thymus gland. Helps with many childhood illnesses, supports weight problems. It stimulates the spleen, adrenal glands and circulation.

EFFECT ON PSYCHE

Rubies have always been considered the lucky stones of the purest form of love. They increase our mental and physical power potential and help even sensitive people to more fulfillment and self-realization. Rubies are inspirational gemstones that represent a high self-esteem. Ruby promotes a zest for life, passion, bravery, virtue and courage. It brings vitality, strength and dynamism and stimulates active sexuality.

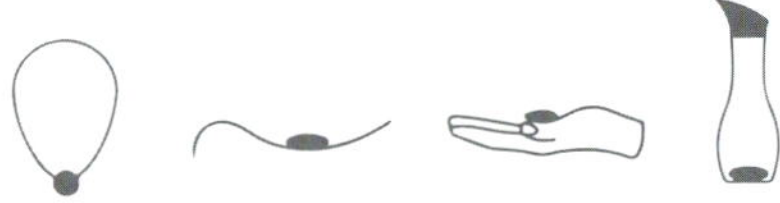

RUTILE QUARTZ

HOPE
IDEAS FOR NEW LIFE CONCEPTS

SIGNIFICANCE

Rutile Quartz is a clear Quartz (can also be Smoky Quartz) with needle-like inclusions of rutile, it belongs to the mineral class of oxides. It has always been considered a truth stone, gives hope, cheers one up and gives us balance as well as vitality. It inspires new ideas and shows new concepts of life.

EFFECT ON THE BODY

Rutile Quartz helps with various diseases of the respiratory tract, especially chronic cough and bronchitis. Our heart and our entire physical regenerative capacity is strengthened by Rutile Quartz. In addition, its use is known for sleep disorders and sexual dysfunctions, such as erectile dysfunction.

EFFECT ON PSYCHE

Rutile Quartz is a powerful stone that has always been revered as a truth and protection stone. With it we can better find our own truth and more self-confidence. It brings us more well-being, harmony and vitality. The protective properties of Rutile quartz warn against evil forces, lies and dishonesty.

SAPPHIRE

MENTAL CLARITY
WILLPOWER
NERVOUS STRENGTH

SIGNIFICANCE

Sapphire is a variety of corundum, it belongs to the mineral class of oxides. It is considered the most effective healing crystal for strengthening the nerves. This gives it a calming effect on the mind. At the same time, the sapphire strengthens the willpower and encourages us to realize our goals or wishes head on. It increases concentration and gives mental clarity.

EFFECT ON THE BODY

Sapphire helps with hair loss, skin diseases, nerve pain, rheumatism, headaches, gout, colic, heartburn, chronic pain, ear ailments, and diseases of the jaw, forehead and sinuses. It strengthens vision, reduces bleeding and sciatic pain. Crystal water with sapphire is said to positively influence even severe health disorders.

EFFECT ON PSYCHE

Sapphire is a healing crystal with high frequency and strong energy. It helps us approach wants, needs and goals with more purpose. It is capable of directing the imagination and the will in such a way that ideas actually become reality. Like few gemstones, it strengthens concentration and improves all mental abilities.

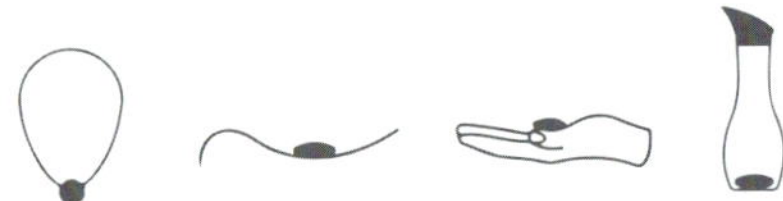

SELENITE

MENTAL STABILITY
CONCENTRATION
CREATIVITY

SIGNIFICANCE

Selenite is formed by desiccation of calcium sulfate and belongs to the mineral class of sulfates. Selenite provides mental stability, soothes the mind and helps with hyperactivity. In addition, selenite increases concentration, provides creativity and gives vitality. It helps to recognize and discard old behavioral patterns.

EFFECT ON THE BODY

Selenite is said to protect reproductive organs such as prostate, testicles, and ovaries. Helps with stomach and digestive problems, flatulence, heartburn, as well as eating disorders. Selenite beneficially stimulates hormone production. It strengthens bones, eases tension in muscles, weakens tension and stress headaches, has a firming and tightening effect on tissues, and can prevent phlebitis and thrombosis.

EFFECT ON PSYCHE

Selenite gives mental stability, releases old behavioral patterns and helps to dissolve them. Dampens a too intense dominance and know-it-all attitude, makes one self-confident and calm. It inspires, gives us vitality and creativity. Selenite strengthens concentration, the interest in important matters and receptivity. In case of oversensitivity, it brings balance and serenity.

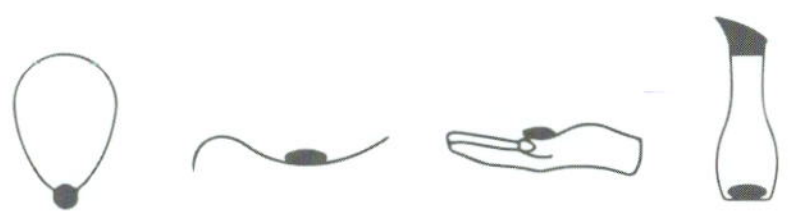

SERPENTINE

INNER PEACE
GOAL ACHIEVEMENT

SIGNIFICANCE

The mineral group serpentine consists of magnesium silicates and belongs to the mineral class of silicates. Serpentine gives a deep inner peace, as it protects and keeps away external influences. In this way it can help with mood swings, balance stress as well as tension and reduce aggressiveness.

EFFECT ON THE BODY

Serpentine strengthens the liver and helps the liver in the body's own detoxification. Serpentine is therefore also popular in diets aimed at holistic detoxification of the human body.

EFFECT ON PSYCHE

Serpentine ensures that the soul of a person again runs in a relaxed way. Strengthens perseverance and helps you to wait for the right moment to make an important decision. It gives people with addiction problems the strength they need to overcome their dependence on harmful substances.

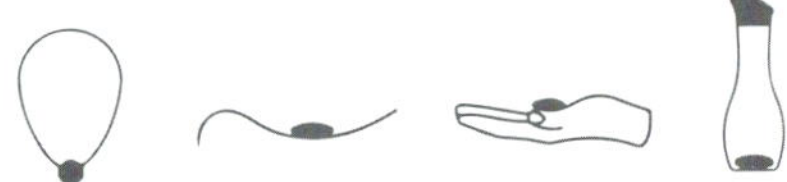

SHUNGITE

VIGOR
VITALITY
HEALTHY SLEEP

SIGNIFICANCE

Shungite consists of 98 percent carbon. Its exceptionally strong life energy acts uniquely to regenerate vitality. It charges the organism with missing energy, which leads to an increase of vitality, normalization of sleep, increase of efficiency and general increase in activity, including sexually.

EFFECT ON THE BODY

Shungite has antibacterial, antiviral, immune system strengthening and anti-inflammatory effects. Appropriate as an antioxidant. It has a supportive effect on osteoarthritis. Used in treatments of bronchial and respiratory diseases, asthma diseases, digestive tract diseases, skin diseases and in treatments of the nervous system. In anti-aging research, Shungite prevailed as an effective "fountain of youth".

EFFECT ON PSYCHE

In order to better process the stimuli in everyday life and thus sleep more relaxed, Shungite is often used. When you carry it with you or drink Shungite water, you feel more comfortable and balanced. Therefore, especially for highly sensitive people, the use of Shungite can represent a positive change.

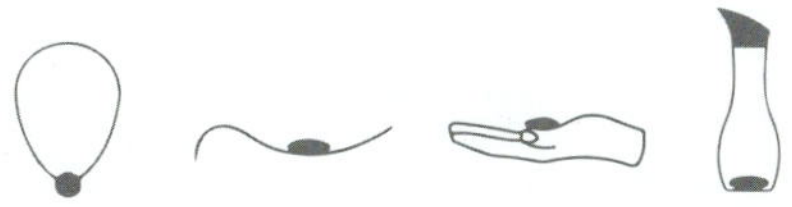

SMOKY QUARTZ

GAIN VITALITY
RELEASE TENSION

SIGNIFICANCE

Smoky Quartz is a smoky brown variety of pure crystal Quartz (Clear Quartz), it belongs to the mineral class of oxides. Smoky Quartz opens the eyes to a new way of life. It restores vitality and helps to cope with grief, depression or even addiction. In addition, smoky quartz allows to relieve inner tension, alleviate the effects of stress and prevent further stress.

EFFECT ON THE BODY

This healing crystal allows scars to heal very well. It corrects postural defects and relieves joint pain. Smoky Quartz can provide the necessary stimulus for physical exercise to an organism weakened by dieting. Thus, this healing crystal can increase the success of a diet.

EFFECT ON PSYCHE

The dark or hazy crystal helps people see clearly into the open future. It counteracts nightmares and is able to release internal blockages. It realigns the social antennae of the soul and ensures active engagement with psychological injuries. Stimulates one to evolve and grow consciously in life.

  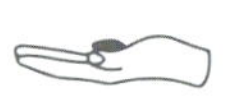  

SODALITE

CLARITY
INTUITION
PERSISTENTLY PURSUING GOALS

SIGNIFICANCE

Sodalite is formed from magma, it belongs to the mineral class of silicates. Sodalite gives you endurance and courage, and at the same time activates self-confidence. It makes you persevere in pursuing goals and increases your thinking power. Stimulates inspiration and intuition.

EFFECT ON THE BODY

With sodalite, the mineral-forming sodium acts on the physical level and primarily stimulates the circulation. It is used to cure rheumatism. It improves cell metabolism and blood circulation. The associated aluminum balances hyperacidity and helps against a state of weakness. It supports and strengthens the pancreas while reducing the risk of diabetes.

EFFECT ON PSYCHE

Sodalite helps to achieve emotional balance and strengthens self-confidence, steadfastness and courage, especially in more sensitive people. It not only activates logical thinking, but also inspires artistic and creative people to create new works. It organizes thoughts and stimulates a well-structured life. Strengthens confidence and idealism. As a volcanic mineral, sodalite helps you to discover and live one's own life.

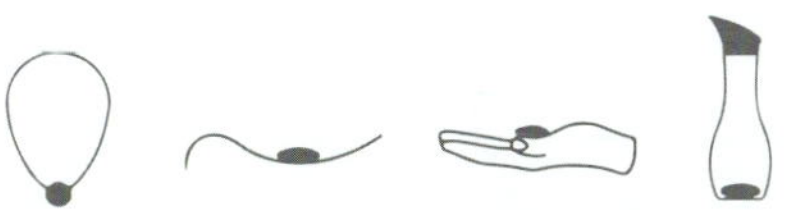

SUGILITE

STRAIGHTFORWARDNESS
PERSONAL RESPONSIBILITY
FEARLESSNESS

SIGNIFICANCE

Sugilite forms metasomatically, it belongs to the mineral class of silicates. It gives us the strength to endure hard times - no matter if it is a stroke of misfortune or drug addiction. Helps with anxiety, paranoia, schizophrenia or grief and significantly supports treatment to overcome these conditions

EFFECT ON THE BODY

Sugilite is a spectacular stone. It has long been associated with serious problems and is considered a good companion for cancer, AIDS and similar serious diseases. It also sharpens all the senses and possibly frees us from fears or helps on the very difficult path out of addictions and dependencies. Those who use a sugilite will definitely have a powerful helper.

EFFECT ON PSYCHE

Sugilite strengthens people who have fallen into dependencies. Mastering crises with an iron will succeeds very well with this liberation stone. Shaping a new life after the strongest illnesses and accidents, for example in a wheelchair, succeeds better with this extraordinary stone. It is especially recommended for phases of disorientation and a search for meaning in life. It gives the will to survive, relieves worries, mental and physical pain, strengthens concentration and helps to always keep your nerves.

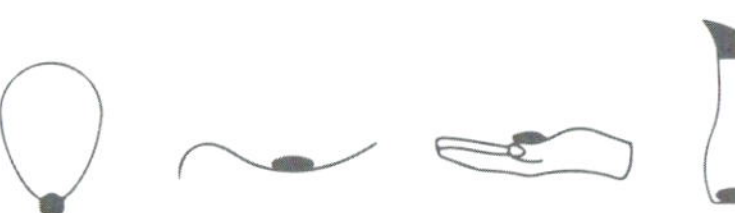

SUNSTONE

GENTLENESS
CONFIDENCE
BALANCE

SIGNIFICANCE

Sunstone is a feldspar. Its characteristic iridescence is caused by inclusions of hematite. The sunstone soothes the mind and has a balancing effect on the psyche. In addition, this healing stone can positively strengthen your own perception.

EFFECT ON THE BODY

Due to its warming properties, the sunstone is a good helper in all disorders of the musculoskeletal system. Joint problems and bone ailments are alleviated with the sunstone and blood circulation is boosted. When the lungs and bronchial tubes are under constant stress, the sunstone is recommended.

EFFECT ON PSYCHE

The sunstone is an illuminating heart stone. It is not only effective against depression, but also strengthens people who feel mentally weak and battered. The sunstone helps you to have a sunny disposition and a good mood. It strengthens a healthy self-esteem and reinforces an alert interest in the environment, at the same time stimulating optimism and a thirst for action.

TANZANITE

CONCENTRATION
LEADERSHIP

SIGNIFICANCE

Tanzanite forms when water accumulates in cavities of gneisses. The blue healing stone strengthens self-confidence and works against lack of concentration. Also actors, teachers and other people who speak professionally in front of an audience have exactly the right help with the blue healing stone.

EFFECT ON THE BODY

Tanzanite contributes to an overall good body feeling and thereby to a self-confident posture. The crystal can also work against headaches. It ensures that the muscles find their way back to a comfortable posture and that more movement becomes enjoyable again. It can show good results in ergotherapeutic measures. A perfect control of one's own body and a self-confident appearance will succeed wonderfully with this stone.

EFFECT ON PSYCHE

Tanzanite is the stone for alpha figures. It strengthens one's own determination and perseverance. It is for people who want to take on leadership roles in the long term. To do this, it liberates us from difficult constellations. With the positive energies of the healing crystal, it is easier to give up old roles and confidently start a new, personal phase of life.

  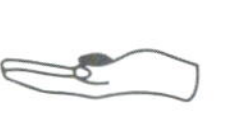   

TIGER'S EYE

COURAGE
BALANCE
SOVEREIGNTY

SIGNIFICANCE

Tiger's Eye is formed during the weathering of falcon's eye. Tiger eye belongs as quartz to the mineral class of oxides. It gives us courage, protection and security. The stone refines the senses and gives distance in cases of ambiguity, allows us to become more serene through greater balance in the face of influences such as stress, strain, doubt or changing moods.

EFFECT ON THE BODY

Tiger's Eye is a powerful healing crystal and is said to strengthen bones and joints, relieves shortness of breath and asthma. Tiger's Eye strengthens the liver, has an antibacterial effect, helps with colds and is bladder and intestinal cleansing. Pain of the musculos-keletal system decreases, joints, back and bones are strengthened and slowly regenerated.

EFFECT ON PSYCHE

Tiger's Eye gives more security. It brings more family warmth, security and balance, and especially increases children's receptive-ness, attention and willingness to learn. For exams, school assignments or driver's license exams, it is recommended to use Tiger's Eye to activate the ability to think clearly and use as a concentration stone.

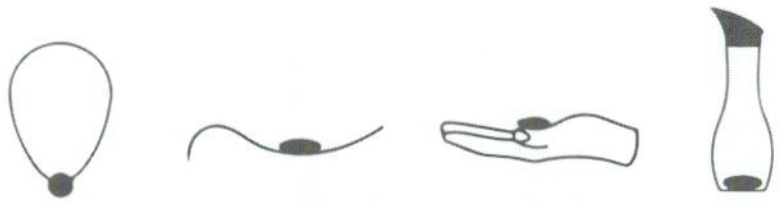

VIRGO

TOPAZ

CONTENTMENT
OPEN-MINDEDNESS
SINCERITY

SIGNIFICANCE

Topaz forms its own group of stones. It is mainly formed during metasomatosis (displacement of one stone by another) and belongs to the mineral class of silicates. Topaz gives us a content and happier emotional life, it stimulates the development of one's abilities. It also bestows upon us an open-minded and sincere nature that can lead to greater success and recognition.

EFFECT ON THE BODY

Topaz helps very well against nausea and hormonal disorders. It calms the nerves, strengthens the heart and blood circulation. Helps with insomnia and exhaustion. Has a positive effect on liver diseases, as well as on nervous headaches, shortness of breath, bronchitis, cough and cold. Topaz also stimulates the taste buds and strengthens the spine.

EFFECT ON PSYCHE

The topaz is known as a lucky stone. It promotes courage and confidence, protects against anxiety, insomnia and depression. Topaz is used in the enhancement of creativity, inspiration and the development of artistic potential. It is said that topaz brings forth unimagined abilities. This stone has a positive effect on nervous-ness and irritability.

  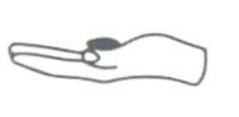 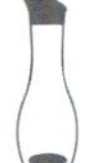  

TOURMALINE BLACK
SCHÖRL

SERENITY
PROTECTION
CREATIVITY

SIGNIFICANCE

Black tourmaline is a mineral group consisting of various mixed crystals, it belongs as borosilicate to the mineral class of silicates. It protects from negative thoughts and influences. It is considered a very strong protective stone against negative energies. It reduces negative thoughts and helps with stress and strain.

EFFECT ON THE BODY

Schörl has a relaxing and pain-relieving effect and helps to neutralize radiation influences. It relieves arthritis, dyslexia, heart disease, and anxiety. It strengthens the muscular, lymphatic and nervous systems. Physically, tourmaline stimulates the energy flow of the meridians and the activity of the entire metabolism. It can therefore be used in all states of weakness and deficiency.

EFFECT ON PSYCHE

Due to its high energetic conductivity and its richness in minerals, tourmaline is a dynamic, uplifting and invigorating healing crystal. It helps to unite the spirit, soul, mind and body into a harmonious unit. It allows us to adopt a calm, neutral attitude, reduces negative thoughts and helps with stress and strain. It also stimulates our creativity.

SCORPIUS

TOURMALINE GREEN
VERDELITE

RENEWAL
NEW WAYS OF THINKING

SIGNIFICANCE

Tourmaline is formed from magma, it belongs as borosilicate to the mineral class of silicates. Verdelite activates hormones and enzymes that are responsible for happiness and satisfaction. It helps to resolve stuck thought patterns. Tourmaline has renewing and rejuvenating properties with an increased effect on family, friendships and partnerships.

EFFECT ON THE BODY

Verdelite strengthens the heart and promotes detoxification. It stimulates the processes of the large intestine and helps against constipation and diarrhea. Green Tourmaline encourages the flow of energy of the meridians and the activity of the entire metabolism. It can therefore be used against al stated of weakness and deficiency symptoms.

EFFECT ON PSYCHE

Traditionally, Green Tourmaline is seen as a manifestation stone for friendships and love. In monotonous life situations, it lends possibilities of reorientation, clarity and flexibility. It helps to rediscover old ideas and goals and encourages to take the next step in life. It helps to relax and can even out mood swings.

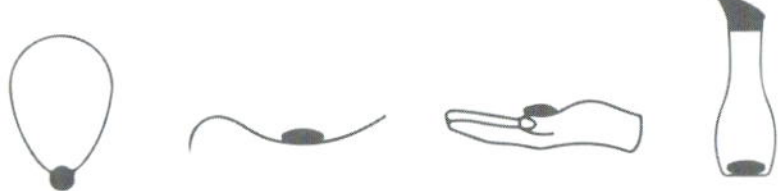

TOURMALINE PINK APYRITE

INNER HARMONY
FINDING SOLUTIONS

SIGNIFICANCE

Tourmaline is formed from magma, it belongs as borosilicate to the mineral class of silicates. Apyrite stimulates inner harmony and an intimate relationship with the environment. It also helps to find a solution to any problem.

EFFECT ON THE BODY

Pink tourmaline helps with vertigo, arthritis, diseases of the nails and nerves, venereal diseases, infertility and menstrual problems. It activates the immune system, detoxifies the liver and protects against X-rays. It stimulates blood circulation and blood purification, as well as the function of the reproductive organs.

EFFECT ON PSYCHE

Pink tourmalines penetrate very strongly into our emotional life and help to better set boundaries. Anxious people who have withdrawn due to disappointments in their relationships or at work receive a positive energy boost. It makes us sociable, charming, promotes ease in life and strengthens the joy of sexuality.

TOURMALINE RED
RUBELLITE

DETERMINATION

SIGNIFICANCE

Tourmaline is formed from magma, it belongs as borosilicate to the mineral class of silicates. Rubellite helps with resolutely pursuing your goals, with overcoming disappointments and with resolving associated pains. It can also restore desire for sexuality.

EFFECT ON THE BODY

Red Tourmaline helps with dizziness, Arthritis, diseases of the nerves, venereal diseases, infertility and menstrual problems. It activates the immune system, detoxifies the liver, stimulates blood circulation and blood purification, strengthens the function of the sexual organs and protects against X-rays.

EFFECT ON PSYCHE

Red tourmalines penetrates our emotional life very strongly and helps to differentiate between compassion and selflessness on the one hand from self-abandonment on the other hand. The red color makes intellectual development more dynamic and flexible.

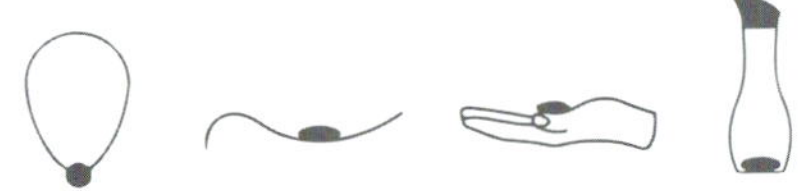

TOURMALINE WATERMELON

SECURITY
LOVE

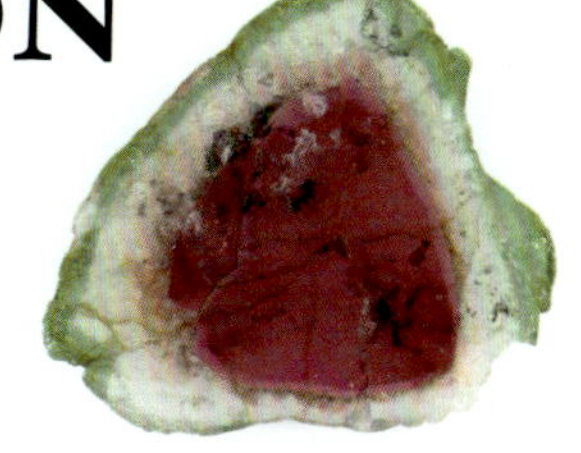

SIGNIFICANCE

Watermelon tourmaline is created either hydrothermal, pneumato-lytic or pneumatically. As a borosilicate, it belongs to the mineral class of silicates. He bestows understanding, love and joy, imparts a feeling of security and brings more self-confidence. Watermelon Tourmaline helps with becoming less aware of prejudices and lessens the symptoms of depression and anxiety

EFFECT ON THE BODY

Watermelon Tourmaline protects against motion sickness and exhaustion. It strengthens the heart and the circulatory system. Healing water mixed with Watermelon Tourmaline is said to be very good for the gums.

EFFECT ON PSYCHE

Watermelon Tourmaline has a liberating effect. It reduces feelings of guilt and melancholy. This tourmaline gives people the self-confidence to take the first step to socialize with others and to seek communication. He frees from test anxiety and lessens existential fears.

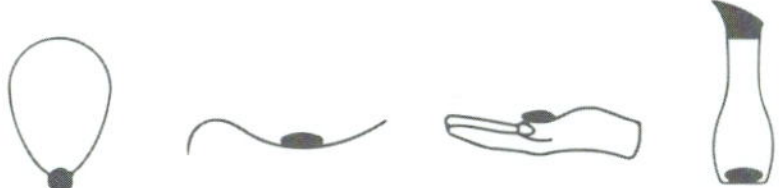

TURQUOISE

PERSEVERANCE
VITALITY
PROTECTION

SIGNIFICANCE

Turquoise is a copper aluminum phosphate. It belongs to the mineral class of phosphates. Turquoise offers protection because it can warn of coming dangers. It helps us to achieve more success, as it strengthens our self-confidence, and improves communication skills. Energy and perseverance increase. It gives the necessary realization that everyone is responsible for his own destiny and gives vitality.

EFFECT ON THE BODY

Turquoise strengthens the liver, all glands, eyes and circulation, it helps with sore throats, and respiratory diseases. Supports therapy against anorexia. Turquoise is used for healing torn ligaments and tendons. Prevents oxygen deficiency and has a positive effect on blood poisoning and stress.

EFFECT ON PSYCHE

Turquoise strengthens reasoning skills and freedom of expression. People who are more reserved should use a turquoise stone to activate their self-confidence. Turquoise conveys more energy and thus supports professional as well as personal success. The turquoise gives us more self-confidence and activates depressed and reserved people.

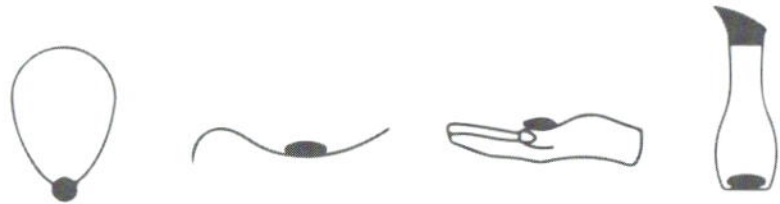

ZIRCONIUM

NO PREJUDICES
DREAMS
SET PRIORITIES

SIGNIFICANCE

Zircon is formed as an early crystallization product primarily in volcanic stones, it belongs to the mineral class of silicates. Zirconium helps with separations or losses. It teaches us to separate the important from the unimportant. In addition, this healing stone frees us from prejudices and rigid life situations. It can inspire new ideas and dreams, and help make them come true.

EFFECT ON THE BODY

The zirconium is found to relieve pain and has a positive effect on menstrual cramps. It has a soothing effect on mucous membranes and relieves hay fever and allergies. It supports the body in diseases of the lungs and bronchi. Hildegard von Bingen attributed zirconium to a fever-reducing and antiseptic effect.

EFFECT ON PSYCHE

Zirconium strengthens self-confidence, reduces feelings of inferiority and self-doubt. It relieves us from sadness and melancholy, and also helps to cope with mental pain. Zirconium inspires the mind, increases one's creativity and inspires us to develop and realize new ideas.

TAURUS   SAGITTARIUS

ZOISITE

SENSE OF REALITY
NEW NEEDS
CREATIVITY

SIGNIFICANCE

Zoisite forms during the metamorphism of calcium-rich stone, it belongs to the mineral class of silicates. Zoisite helps with mental stress, depression and aggressiveness. This healing stone increases the sense of reality and guards against recklessness or rash actions. Zoisite gives you creativity and makes you look for new needs or ideas.

EFFECT ON THE BODY

A stone for the reproductive organs: so it can protect against possible venereal diseases and is said to increase fertility. It also promotes blood circulation and supports the cardiovascular system. It works against overexertion or general flabbiness and gives a whole new body feeling.

EFFECT ON PSYCHE

Zoisite leads emotional states into a new state of consciousness. This makes it easier to assess one's own feelings, which can be a great advantage in certain life situations where important decisions have to be made. It helps to achieve a higher degree of creativity. For artistic production or the development of one's personality, zoisite is a good companion.

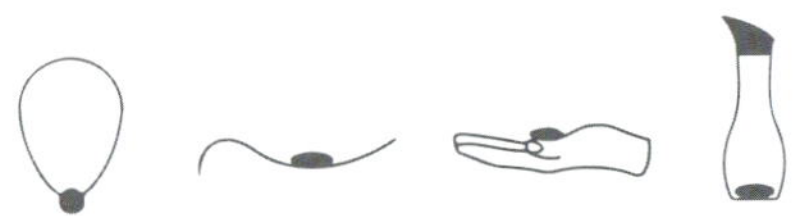

HELPFUL GEMSTONES
PHYSICAL

INDICATION	++	+
Acne	Aventurine	Peridot
Abdomen	Red Jasper	Carnelian
Anorexia	Sugilite	Amethyst
Back pain	Green Calcite	Hematite
Bile	Red Jasper	Heliotrope
Birth	Red Jasper	Agate
Blood composition, cleansing	Hematite	Carnelian
Bones	Calcite, all colors	Aragonite
Bronchial tubes	Rutile Quartz	Amber
Burns	Green Calcite	Hematite
Cervical vertebrae	Green Calcite	Chrysocolla
Cold	Amber	Aquamarine
Cough	Amber	Chalcedony
Cramps	Amazonite	Malachite
Detoxify	Malachite	Carnelian
Diaphragm	Rutile Quartz	Citrine
Digestion	Red Jasper	Carnelian
Ears	Amber	Onyx
Eyes	Emerald	Clear Quartz
Eyesight	Falcon's Eye	Beryl

INDICATION	++	+
Feet, cold	Snowflake Obsidian	
Fertility	Chrysoprase	Garnet
Flatulence	Red Jasper	
Flu	Rutile Quartz	Heliotrope
Frontal sinusitis	Amber	Sapphire
Gout	Green Calcite	Amber
Growth, physical	Calcite	Aragonite
Hay fever	Amber	Carnelian
Headache	Amethyst	Dumortierite
Headache / migraine	Rhodochrosite	
Heart, general	Rose Quartz	Chrysoprase
Heartburn	Rutile Quartz	Spinel
Hormonal disorders	Chalcedony	Clear Quartz
Immune System	Sugilite	Heliotrope
Impotence	Garnet	
Increase blood pressure	Garnet	Hematite
Infertility	Garnet	Chrysoprase
Inflammations	Malachite	
Intestine, general	Red Jasper	Carnelian
Joints (pain)	Green Calcite	Amber
Kidneys	Heliotrope	Jade
Liver	Red Jasper	Malachite
Lower blood pressure	Lapis Lazuli	Sodalite
Lumbago	Hematite	Amber

INDICATION	++	+
Lungs	Rutile Quartz	Amber
Lymph nodes	Clear Quartz	Aquamarine
Menopause	Chalcedony	Moonstone
Menstrual problems	Red Jasper	Moonstone
Metabolism	Citrine	Peridot
Nausea	Clear Quartz	
Neck tension	Chrysocolla	
Nervous System	Clear Quartz	Rutile Quartz
Neurodermatitis	Aventurine	Peridot
Nosebleeds	Carnelian	Amber
Osteoarthritis	Green Calcite	Amber
Perspiration	Chalcedony	Moonstone
Poisoning	Malachite	Chrysoprase
Pregnancy	Agate	Red Jasper
Prostate	Mix of 4minerals	Black Tourmaline
Reduce cholesterol levels	Magnesite	
Regulate blood circulation	Rhodocrosite	Rhodonite
Respiratory tract, asthma	Amber	Aquamarine
Rheumatism	Amber	Malachite
Scars	Hematite	Sugilite
Sciatica	Green Calcite	Hematite
Sex organs	Garnet	Carnelian
Sexual problems	Chrysoprase	Agate
Sinus infection	Sapphire	Amber

INDICATION	++	+
Skin	Aventurine	Peridot
Sore throat	Amber	Chalcedony
Spine	Green Calcite	Magnetite
Stimulate blood circulation	Garnet	Ruby
Stomach	Agate	Emerald
Strengthen blood circulation	Garnet	Hematite
Strengthen teeth	Calcite	Fluorite
Stroke	Diamond	
Swellings	Lapis Lazuli	
Teething children / babies	Amber	
Tendons	Green Calcite	Amber
Tension	Amazonite	Chrysocolla
Thyroid gland	Clear Quartz	Chalcedony
Tinnitus	Black Tourmaline	
Tonsils	Aquamarine	Amber
Toothache	Amber	Aquamarine
Varicose veins	Amethyst	Magnesite
Veins	Hematite	Amethyst
Vocal cords	Chalcedony	Topaz
Warts	Lapis Lazuli	Turquoise
Water retention	Aquamarine	Magnesite
Womb	Agate	Red Jasper
Wounds, physically	Hematite	Rhodonite

HELPFUL GEMSTONES
MENTAL

INDICATION	++	+
Alleviate exam anxiety	Azurite	Chalcedony
Alleviate inner turmoil	Amethyst	Rose Quartz
Alleviate nervousness	Amethyst	Aventurine
Promote creativity	Lapis lazuli	Onyx
Boost self-confidence	Sodalite	
Build up protection	Tourmaline Black	Turquoise
Conquer panic	Amethyst	Rhodonite
Enjoy relaxation	Chrysoprase	Amazonite
Erase negative thoughts	Tourmaline Black	
Feeling secure	Agate	Tiger's Eye
Gain clarity	Clear Quartz	Amethyst
Gain serenity	Chalcedony	Larimar
Gain zest for life	Fuchsite	Labradorite
Give up smoking	Botswana Agate	Smoky Quartz
Grieving	Smoky Quartz	Rutile Quartz
Healing mental wounds	Rhodonite	Malachite
Improve kindness	Rose Quartz	
Improve perception	Sodalite	Azurite
Improve perseverance	Onyx	Smoky Quartz

INDICATION	++	+
Improve relationship	Milk Quartz	
Improve speaking ability, fluency of speech	Chalcedony	
Improve stamina	Garnet	Ruby
Increase energy	Garnet	Ruby
Intensify creativity	Fire Opal	Imperial Topaz
Learning disability/ learning stress	Fluorite	Azurite
Make a new start/ turn your life around	Sugilite	Amethyst
Making decisions	Azurite	Fluorite
Overcome addictions	Amethyst	Sugilite
Overcome fear	Amethyst	Rhodonite
Overcome feeling of inferiority	Sodalite	Lapis Lazuli
Overcome inhibitions	Chalcedony	Sodalite
Peaceful sleep, falling asleep well	Amethyst	Rose Quartz
Prevent/cure depression	Citrine	Lapis Lazuli
Reduce aggression	Rose Quartz	Amethyst
Reduce anger, rage	Amethyst	Howlite
Reduce emotional hardness	Rose quartz	Moonstone
Reduce fatigue	Garnet	Ruby
Reduce feelings of guilt	Sodalite	

INDICATION	++	+
Reduce signs of fatigue	Garnet	Ruby
Reduce speech disorders & stuttering	Chalcedony	Amethyst
Remove blockages	Clear Quartz	Chrysoprase
Shock/Trauma processing	Smoky Quartz	Rutile Quartz
Soothe Irritability & Temper	Rose Quartz	Amethyst
Stimulate spiritual growth	Moldavite	Lapis Lazuli
Strengthen compassion & empathy	Rose Quartz	Moonstone
Strengthen inner peace	Rose Quartz	Agate
Strengthen memory	Fluorite	Lapis Lazuli
Stress reduction	Amethyst	Citrine

CRYSTAL
WATER

THE LARGEST WATER TREATMENT PLANT ON EARTH

All around the world, millions of wastewater treatment plants and waterworks purify our water 24 hours a day, so we can enjoy it without any health risks.

However, by far the largest recycling of water on our planet is Mother Nature itself. It regenerates our water energetically and in a healthy way. We can enjoy this excellent water at any source. It flows from springs into creeks, from there into rivers and finally ends up in lakes or water reservoirs. We have learned that, water is not used up, there is no "new water" coming from anywhere. Instead it is polluted and recycled in a constant cycle:

WATER IS CONSTANTLY BEING POLLUTED AND RECYCLED WORLDWIDE

Water evaporates.

Giant clouds form.

Water rains down on the earth and seeps into the ground.

Stones in the soil revitalize and regenerate our water.

Energetic and healthy, it emerges again at natural springs.

We all know that spring water has the highest quality of all water types anywhere on our planet. It happens all by itself, no one has to bring the water into the earth and we don't need to invest any energy in recycling it. It works so simple because nature has arranged it that way. Therefore, we can take advantage of the simple principle of nature:

ELEMENT STONES REGENERATES ELEMENT WATER

CRYSTAL WATER
A NEW OPPORTUNITY
FOR OUR HEALTH

Many thousands of foods and plants have not been scientifically tested for their effectiveness. Yet we recognize that they are good for us. We also feel both fitter and healthier when we consume them. Has honey ever been thoroughly scientifically studied for its health effects? Not to my knowledge, yet everyone knows how healthy and healing honey is. Just like everyone who drinks crystal water every day and experiences its effects firsthand. Every day you feel and sense how beneficial and healthy high-energy water is for your life:

- increased sense of well-being
- less infections
- higher immunity
- better sleep
- better skin
- better metabolism
- more performance
- better concentration and learning ability
- higher memory performance

These are the most essential changes that crystal water drinkers notice in their daily lives. Why does crystal water have such an effect? It is because water makes up the majority of our body and we clearly perceive the influence of good water on every aspect of our daily life - when relaxing, sleeping, or working.

When you reflect on it, it will become totally obvious to you. Stones give the water a beneficial and healthy molecular structure, gemstones even more intensely than ordinary stones. Water absorbs this information and stores it for a certain period of time. The reason for the remarkable effect of crystal water is because the information of the stones stimulates the memory of water. Water is a natural element and has been informed with stones since the existence of our planet, so it has this healthy information in its memory.

Gemstones pass their primal information on to water. Water absorbs this information, which provides essential corrections in the body towards increased well-being, better health and longer active life.

Decisive for the effect of crystal water is the arrangement of the molecules in the water. Researchers at Oxford University in England have investigated how vital a healthy molecular structure is for a healthy food, and even how it can make a difference between life and death. Newborn calves are suckled by the mother cow with her maternal milk. In an Oxford study, normal cow's milk was pasteurized, i.e. it was briefly heated to about 70 degrees Celsius, which changed the molecular structure. Newborn calves that drank this pasteurized milk did not survive three weeks. So much for the effect of a fundamentally altered food on a mammal's organism.

INFORMATION DETERMINES AND CONTROLS ENERGY.
ENERGY DETERMINES AND CONTROLS MATTER

Since water is the most important food for us humans, a healthy molecular structure in water has particularly positive effects on health, fitness, well-being and many more.

THE MOLECULAR STRUCTURE OF OUR FOOD DETERMINES WHETHER WE ARE HEALTHY OR SICK - WHETHER WE LIVE OR DIE.

Some companies sell their own self-programmed energizing systems for water. Information that is usually applied to silicon wafers or transferred via magnets. They are modified accordingly by a human mind. However, as we have often experienced, no human being, no computer can even come close to simulating the force of nature. Only nature provides the optimal molecular structure, nothing and no one can improve this process. We have experienced many times in the past what disastrous effects human manipulations can have on nature. We all get to see the disastrous effects of fracking, how nuclear fission threatens our entire livelihood or how river straightening causes devastating floods.

A great advantage of crystal water is that the effect of the stones is not limited to specific parts of the body, but always encompasses the entire body.

At the same time, gemstones fundamentally improve the water quality of our drinking water:

- They keep drinking water fresh and improve the taste.
- They neutralize negative consequences of mechanical drinking water treatment.
- They revive "dead water" that has been destroyed by very high pressure and toxins in the pipes.
- They stimulate the bioavailability of nutrients dissolved in water and their vital properties.
- They are suitable to produce special medicinal waters.

NOTHING CAN SHAPE WATER IN A HEALTHIER AND MORE ENERGETIC WAY THAN GEMSTONES.

Laboratory results
on crystal water

Several institutes have scientifically analyzed crystal water.

The international research laboratory Hagalis in Überlingen on Lake Constance has compared crystal water to regular tap water and made sensational results:

- Significant improvement in tap water quality.
- Neutralization of all contaminant information.
- Improvement of the pH value and the oxygen content.
- Improved bioavailability of minerals.
- Increased vitality.

Evidence of contaminants under the microscope:

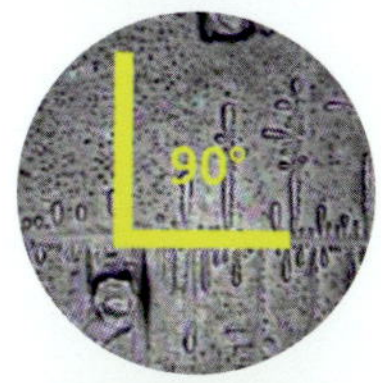

Biologists can see from the molecular arrangement whether pollutants are contaminating matter. Pollutants can be identified when molecular structures are arranged at a 90° angle.

In nature, pollutant-free, uncontaminated molecules always arrange themselves at a 60-degree angle.

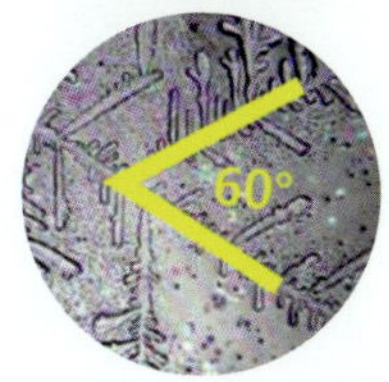

The image of the crystal water molecules under the microscope clearly shows natural, pollutant-free and uncontaminated molecular arrangement. This is proof that crystal water neutralizes contaminant information.

Summary evaluation from the Hagalis analysis institute:

Both from a biological and nutritional point of view, there has been a significant increase in water quality after gemstone treatment. Compared to the neutral sample (tap water), there is a significant increase in quality. This enables the water sample to reach a quality level that is otherwise only known from spring water.

CRYSTAL WATER NEUTRALIZES ALL POLLUTANT INFORMATION.

Hado Laboratory, Tokyo

The world-famous HADO Institute in Tokyo has also conducted studies of crystal water. It continues the life's work of Dr. Masaru Emoto. The laboratory freezes water at minus 30 degrees Celsius and photographs the thawing water droplet with an electron microscope.

Normal tap water and crystal water were photographed:

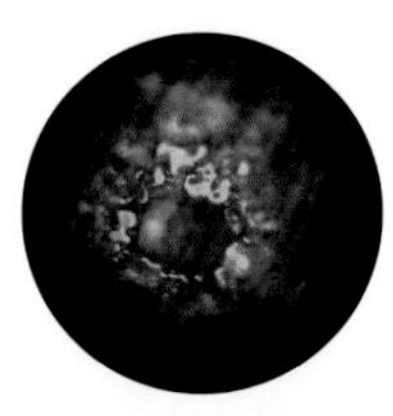

Tap water from Tokyo

Crystal water

I believe these pictures do not need any further commenting. You can imagine how well crystal water benefits the body and has a positive effect on it.

Further proof that stones influence our water: Many mineral water companies obtain their water from rocky areas. Here are a few examples:

San Pellegrino
Spring in Val Brembana at the foothills of the Italian Alps

Evian
Spring in the heart of the French Alps in Evian-les-Bains

Volvic
Spring in the French Auvergne under the volcano "Puy de Dome".

Plose
Spring in Brixen near the -Dolomites, South Tirol

Gerolsteiner
Spring in the Volcanic Eifel, Germany

Vitell
Spring in the Vosges, France

Adelholzener
Spring in the Bavarian Alps, Germany

THE SPRINGS OF ALL WELL-KNOWN MINERAL WATER COMPANIES ORIGINATE IN "ROCKY" MOUNTAINS.

WINE AND GEMSTONES

By pure chance I discovered the effect of gemstones on wine. A winemaker friend, Augusto from Italy, owns a beautiful winery in Emilia-Romagna and invited me to visit him. At a wine tasting in the evening, I took an amethyst, which I always carry with me, out of my pocket and put it in my wine glass. This evening will not be forgotten by everyone involved, because after about ten minutes the Sangiovese tasted much milder, the typical tannin, that is, the substance that makes the wine somewhat bitter, had disappeared completely. It seemed like the amethyst reduced the tannins and enhanced the fruit flavors. This experience was like a revelation. My friend was so enthusiastic that the following weekend he invited all the winemaking colleagues from the association to a sensory wine tasting. I was also still a guest in this round, we were all surprised on one side and enormously pleased on the other side. Back home, I naturally wanted to know if there was a reasonable background for this and did more research. In the ancient Greek language Amethyst means "the non-intoxicable". For explanation, methods of wine growers from Greece about 5000 years ago were mentioned. At that time they poured wine over the Amethyst and noticed similar phenomena as we did 5000 years later in Imola. If you look at the powers of gemstones, the effect is easy to explain: Since wine is 99 percent water and gemstones re-inform water molecules, it is naturally clear that gemstones also change the wine.

AMETHYST MAKES WINE SOFTER AND FRUITIER

For me and my "gemstone friends" it was once again a fantastic confirmation, as this transformation of the molecular arrangement can be tasted even more intensively in wine than in water. Of course, you can't conjure up the bouquet of a "wine of the century" from a mediocre wine. However, the change in taste is so intense that anyone, even with a low sensory level of the tongue and palate, can taste this transformation and enjoy the rich fruitiness of the wine.

VitaJuwel - Wine decanter & Gemstone Vial Vino

> *„He who drinks wine sleeps well, he who sleeps well„*
> *does not sin, he who does not sin is blessed,*
> *so he who drinks wine is blessed."*
>
> — William Shakespeare —

VitaJuwel - Gemstone Droplet Amethyst

> *„What is life's highest pleasure?*
> *Love and wine."*
>
> Joachim Perinet

PLANTS AND CRYSTAL WATER

Water is the primary component of all plants. In the floral world, water is an indispensable electron donor and reaction partner in photosynthesis. Water is above all responsible for the transport for nutrient salts and for assimilates formed by the plant to the correspondingly important locations. These functions of the water molecule make it clear that an adequate supply of water to the plant organism is the most important prerequisite for its survival.

With crystal water being the most natural of all consumable waters, it was exciting to discover if this water would have an impact on the growth, durability and appearance of plants.

Mishari Al Faraj runs an exclusive flower shop in Kuwait City.

The store sells hundreds of bouquets every day, and also decorates exclusive homes with floristry. Many big events are furnished with flower arrangements by Al Faraj.

For years, he has been researching in his lab how different waters affect flowers, especially whether water can affect longevity.

An experiment he conducted with bamboo plants and roses in crystal water yielded astonishing results: Roses in tap water developed brown edges after only four days, whereas the roses in crystal water still looked fresh and healthy after seven days. The bamboo in tap water turned brown after a week. In crystal water, however, the bamboo even formed new roots after a week!

While Mishari Al Farad's results are sensational, I expected them to be so. Crystal water strengthens Flowers, prolongs their flowering time and makes flowers bloom beautifully Plants have no design sensibility, do not respond to the placebo effect, and of course, do not have human emotional sensibility. Nevertheless, crystal water acts in a completely natural way. It extends their life and gives them an unprecedented appearance. This is another way of showing how great nature is in enriching our lives.

WITH CYSTAL WATER CUT FLOWERS BLOOM LONGER AND ARE MORE BEAUTIFUL.

THE "SEVENTH SENSE" OF ANIMALS

Have you noticed that dogs love to drink water from puddles, streams or lakes when they're out walking? Would we do the same?

No way! Why not? Because we don't have the sensory system that animals have. An animal is an outright opportunist, because all of its actions always have a single goal: "How am I doing better?" So within the spectrum of their instincts, they also have the instinct to recognize the best water for themselves. Cats, like dogs, have this instinct.

ANIMALS HAVE A NATURAL INSTINCT FOR HEALTHY WATER.

We have two Bichon Frisé dogs living with us, two males, Picco and Tiger. If we are not careful, they will jump on the table and drink from our crystal water glasses. After we noticed this, we gave them crystal water from our decanter into their drinking bowl. In the process, we noticed a great change: Picco used to have problems with dehydration. Our vet recommended that we keep spraying water between his lips with a syringe so he could get his water that way. Since we have been giving our dogs crystal water to drink, Picco also drinks like a world champion.

Friends of ours have a cat and they also drink crystal water. The other day, our friend told us that her cat had repeatedly knocked over and broke the crystal water decanter out of greed.

In animals, the dominant portion of body mass is water, and healthy water has a similar effect on their health as it does on ours. Now our vet also drinks crystal water and she also recommends it to her clients/patients. Recently, she shared that she had been constantly treating a female dog for her kidney problems. For almost two months now the mutt has also been drinking crystal water and the kidney problems have almost disappeared.

No life without water. This motto does not only apply to humans, animals are also subject to this principle of nature. For all metabolic processes to run normally and function smoothly, the water content in the animals' bodies must be right. Even small fluctuations can extremely limit the performance or even lead to the collapse of the entire system.

Many pets do not like fresh tap water, according to the animal welfare organization PETA. It is better to use clean rainwater or crystal water. Especially cats like running water - a drinking fountain with stones can be useful.

If you suspect your pet is not drinking enough or is even dehydrated, there are a few tests you can do. Do not rely on the temperature or humidity of the nose. The mucous membranes should be moist and pink. When dehydrated, they become dry and sticky. If you slowly pull up the skin in the shoulder and neck area to form a wrinkle, it should immediately return to normal when you release it. If the wrinkle is slow to recede or does not recede at all, the animal is dehydrated and needs more water.

If an animal is not drinking as much as it should, it could be that the water is finicky. You should provide the animal with a sufficient amount of fresh water at all times and change the water at least once a day - preferably crystal water, of course. On average, an animal should drink about 2 fl.oz. per kilogram (=2.2 lbs) of body mass daily.

VitaJuwel offers a drinking bowl for pets. Prior to the launch, the company has conducted tests on 200 animals. The animals were offered two drinking bowls, one with regular tap water and the other with crystal water. In 200 out of 200 choices, cats and dogs preferred crystal water. When the company ships drinking bowls, they include a note recommending that the new drinking bowl be placed next to the one previously used. Their customer feedback confirms that the animals now drink exclusively from the crystal water bowl.

„When the goose sees water, its tail wags.“
— German proverb —

PREPARATION OF
CRYSTAL WATER

To prepare crystal water, you need gemstones of your own choice (information about their respective effects are in the gemstone section), water and a container, preferably a glass decanter. For water, you can use spring water if available, mineral water or tap water.

Although there are basically no limits to the use of healing crystals for the preparation of crystal water, and the production of crystal water is seemingly simple. But there are some specifics that should be taken into account:

- You should check the individual stones carefully in advance, because some stones can release toxic substances into the drinking water. In case of doubt, it is better not to use a stone or mixtures for crystal water or to work with an alternative manufacturing process. Here is an overview of stones that are not suitable for the production of crystal water (without claim to completeness):

  - Turquoise
  - Azurite
  - Malachite
  - Fluorite
  - Vanadinite
  - Cinnabar

- The number of individual stones within the same container should not exceed seven varieties.

- For the selection of gemstone blends the mineralogical relationship and as many matching properties of the individual stone varieties as possible should be taken into account. You can select stones in different ways:

The empirical way

Stones that you've had special experiences with before come first here. At the same time, there is a large selection of literature where you can acquire new knowledge about stones. Maybe you have people in your circle of friends and acquaintances who already have gemstone experience - you can also consult with them.

The intuitive way

It is best to use the stones that are particularly appealing to you, that seem beneficial to you, or that feel pleasant to the touch. This path, which has often led us successfully with our "gut feeling", can also support you when choosing stones.

The analytical way

This requires knowledge about the formation, structure, and substance and color effect of a stone. Scientists from analytical crystal healing are the right people to contact for this purpose. Experts in crystal healing oftentimes give very detailed information in various publications.

I would like to recommend two authors in particular:

Walter von Holst, Steinkreis Stuttgart
Michael Gienger, Tübingen, d. 2014

**THERE ARE SEVERAL WAYS
TO FIND THE PERFECT GEMSTONE**

Preparing crystal water step by step

The first step is to clean the gemstones impeccably, under running water with a brush. You may even want to boil them so the stone does not contain any toxic substances.

Then put the stone in a container and pour water over it. After about one to two hours, or possibly longer, you can enjoy pure, healthy crystal water.

After two to three days, a layer of mucus forms around the stones, which may contain germs. Therefore, they must be removed and cleaned again at regular intervals.

One should be careful when drinking, because it can happen again and again that splinters come off the stones, which then float in the water and are possibly ingested with the water.

Test tube method

Since stones work through their electromagnetic frequencies, 100% information transfer through the glass into the water is guaranteed.

To prepare crystal water using the test tube method, you need a suitable test tube and the respective water stones in an appropriate size. You simply place them in the test tube. Place the test tube with the water stones in a glass jug or in a glass with spring water, mineral water or tap water. In addition to mini stones or other small water stones, gemstones that are unsuitable for direct insertion into water can also be placed in the test tube. These include porous gemstones. Tests have demonstrated that the gemstone effect is fully achieved in two to three hours.

Gemstone plates as coasters for glass

With a gemstone plate as a glass coaster it is very easy to prepare crystal water. Indirect contact with the stone prevents toxic, oiled or waxed stones from contaminating the water. Unfortunately, the choice of suitable gemstone coasters is very limited. Also the informing of the water takes much longer than with the direct insertion of the stones or with the test tube method or the VitaJuwel method.

Water in gemstone bowls

Gemstones or minerals that have an appropriate size or stability are suitable for bowls. This is one of the simplest methods of preparing crystal water. Unfortunately, the amount of water is limited by the size of the bowl. The information transfer succeeds in a similar time as when the stones are placed directly into the water.

Initiation with Clear Quartz

Naturally grown and untreated clear quartz acts like lasers: they absorb information at the base and sides and direct it to the top. Now, if you place a stone at the base of the clear quartz and point the tip at a container of water, the information from the stone will quickly flow into the water. If possible, the crystal should not have any opacities, i.e. it should be almost clear and should not be polished on the sides and the tip.

You can put the water container preferably on a natural wooden plate and put the crystal on the side with the tip to the container. The information transfer time is four to six times shorter than when stones are placed in water. Another advantage is that the gemstones have no direct contact with the water.

The VitaJuwel method

In the traditional method of making crystal water, the gemstones are placed directly into the drinking water. In this case, the stones should be thoroughly cleaned and disinfected before first use to remove contamination. The gemstones should also be cleaned and disinfected regularly at short intervals for further use, otherwise they will germinate or release undesirable dirt particles. Despite careful cleaning, especially stones with a low degree of hardness can regularly release substances into the drinking water, which are then also consumed. With the VitaJuwel method, you no longer need to worry about this. The gemstones used at VitaJuwel are tumbled and cleaned several times in a special ultrasonic process before they are used. They are then filled into the VitaJuwel vials and bottles, in which they float gently and well-sealed in a solution specially developed for this purpose.

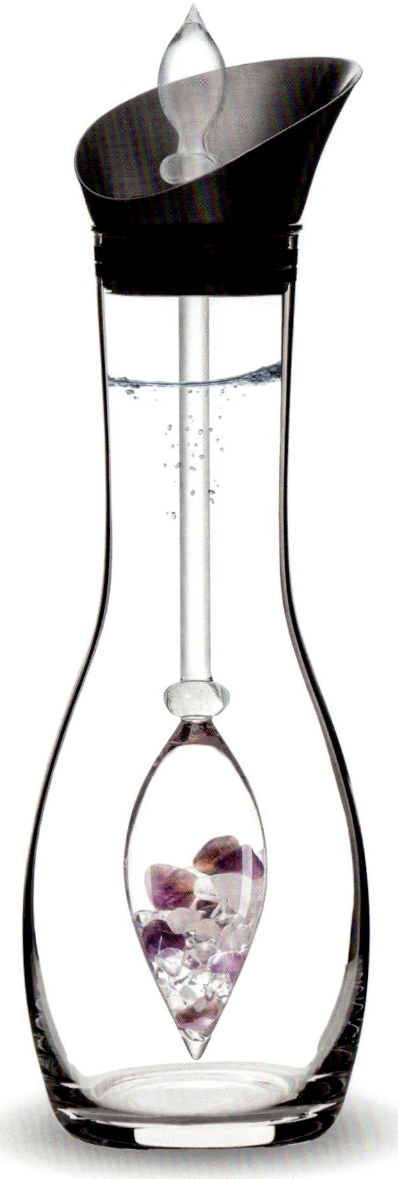

The advantages of the VitaJuwel method

- The gemstones no longer need to be placed directly into the water.
- VitaJuwel protects drinking water from possible contamination by gemstones or from stone fragments.
- There is no need for time-consuming cleaning of the gemstones.
- VitaJuwel is hygienic. In 2008, the method was awarded the Gastro Vision Award as the most hygienic way to prepare crystal water.
- High quality, virtually unbreakable borosilicate glass is used.
- The gemstones are selected all over the world by gemstone specialists and cleaned in a multi-stage purification process.
- When selecting the stones, not only the quality plays a role; attention is also paid to whether all social aspects at the mines are guaranteed and the Fairtrade guidelines are complied with.
- VitaJuwel offers ready-made mixtures that have blended by experts in crystal healing, gemologists and water sommeliers.
- The results are unprecedented; within seven minutes the water is fully informed. The reasons are, on the one hand, the quality of the stones, the solution in which the gemstones float, and the shape of the containers, which allow for a focused transmission of information.
- Ultimately, the aesthetically designed containers encourage a positive awareness of water, inspiring us to drink more. At the same time, we know that when we drink, our consciousness can influence the effect on the body.

The VitaJuwel bottle also gives you the extraordinary opportunity to enjoy crystal water on the go. The bottle can be opened both at the top and at the bottom. This makes it easy to clean and you can insert and use different gemstone modules as needed. The idea of VitaJuwel was conceived in 2007.

Meanwhile, millions of enthusiastic people enjoy this method. Decanters or bottles by VitaJuwel can be found in good hotels or spas, at holistic therapists and medical practitioners, in fitness and cosmetic studios, in retail stores and, of course, in many private households.

> *„VitaJuwel is the most hygienic method to prepare crystal water.“*
>
> — Ewald Eisen

Recently, VitaJuwel has also started offering pump and spray bottles for body oils or refreshing waters. I use this range for my cooking oil and vinegar, the effect of the stones on the oils or on the vinegar is sensational. The vinegar bottle contains amethysts, my vinegar is as mild as a very mild balsamic, similarly to wine, the amethyst takes the sharpness and bitterness and promotes all the fruit flavors. I can still taste the flavor of my olive oil even on the single lettuce leaf, so intensely does the flavor of the oil develop. Thus, even in the culinary segment, It becomes apparent how gemstones have an effect on the surrounding media.

> *„This is the true joy in life: Being used for a purpose recognized by yourself as a mighty one.“*
>
> —— George Bernard Shaw ——

SYMBOLS

The following blends are commercially
available in the varieties listed below:

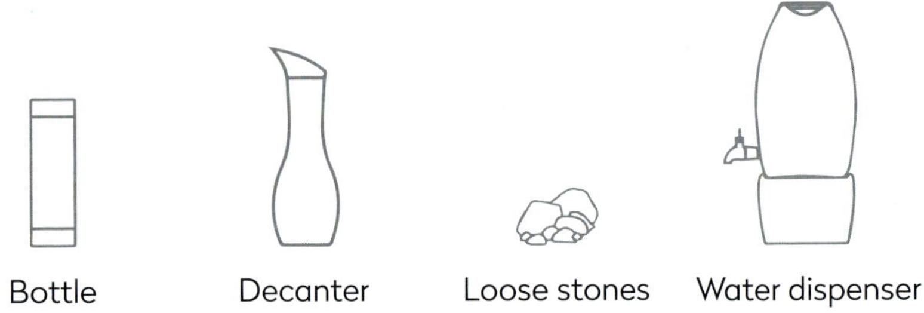

CHAKRA ENERGY CENTERS

With Chakra (Sanskrit for "wheel" or "circle") in Hinduism, also in Yoga the assumed original energy centers between the physical body and the ethereal body of the human being are described. According to this teaching, both bodies are connected by energy channels.

Indian chakra teachings include seven chakras. The seven main chakras are of special importance and represent the whole spectrum of our life themes. The chakras are in constant circular motion, which causes energy to be drawn into the heart of the chakras.

They are nodes for the soul and the body. This is also the origin of the realization that the soul, when it suffers, can make the body ill. If only one of these chakras is blocked, the entire flow of energy may be obstructed. When chakras are strongly developed and free of such blockages as much as possible, they appear open and radiate their energy intensely.

Blockages often mature unnoticed over years insidiously and can prevent happiness because they significantly affect character and health. They often cause increasing pessimism and anxiety and, if not treated, inevitably lead to physical ailments.

Gemstones can dissolve existing negative blockages and thus regenerate the body. Chakra-active gemstones have proven to be safe helpers for thousands of years.

Therefore, in my recommendations I discuss the effect of the gemstones and especially the crystal water and mention the chakra recommendation as an additional note.

SPECIAL CRYSTAL WATER
RECIPES

WELLNESS

AMETHYST

ROSE QUARTZ

CLEAR QUARTZ

PROPERTIES

This well-balanced composition has already been used for several hundreds of years to inspirit water by countless people all around the world. Experts claim that amethyst stimulates the mind and soothes emotions. Rose Quartz fosters tranquility and harmony. Clear Quartz is a stone for clarity and perception. As a combination, they're used for their wonderfully invigorating effect.

 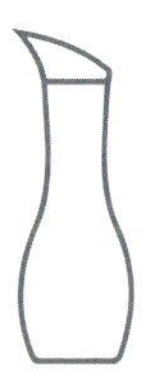 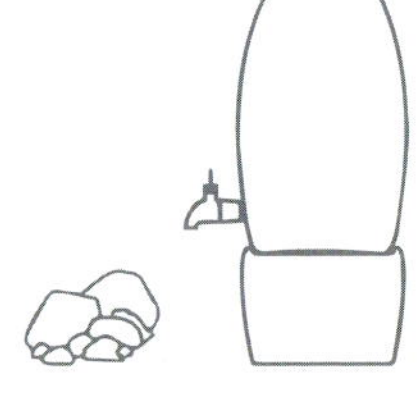   

FITNESS

JASPER RED

MAGNESITE

CLEAR QUARTZ

PROPERTIES

Drinking water first thing in the morning is an easy way to speed up your metabolism. Lots of people confuse thirst for hunger, so staying hydrated could help you avoid overeating. Make a start, put on your running shoes and fill your water bottle with "Fitness" crystal elixir. Include this special blend in your regular workout schedule and get ready for a surprise!

FIVE ELEMENTS

AMETHYST

ROSE QUARTZ

CHALCEDONY

PETRIFIED WOOD

OCEAN AGATE

PROPERTIES

Traditional Chinese medicine has developed over 5,000 years and sees health as a harmonious balance of five elements: Wood for growth, water for reflection, earth for grounding, metal for strength and fire for passion. Every person is a unique blend of these elements. Following this ancient philosophy, there is one kind of gem for each element in this blend to reflect each attribute.

BALANCE

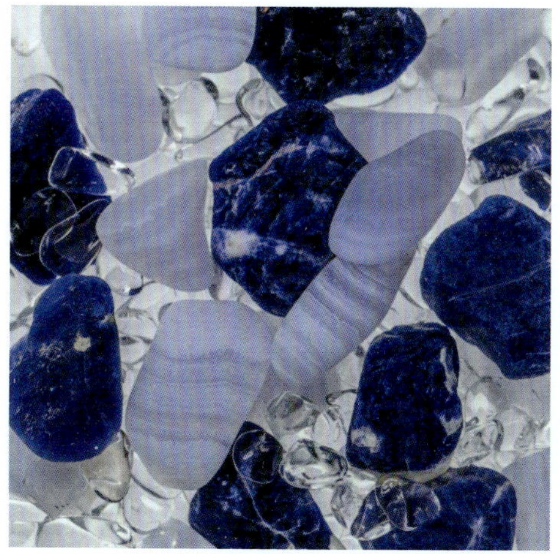

SODALITE

CHALCEDONY BLUE

CLEAR QUARTZ

PROPERTIES

Sodalite is traditionally used by crystal healing experts to support mental balance, calmness and inner peace. It's said to support expressing your thoughts and is therefore also known as the Poet's Stone. This attribute is wonderfully complemented by blue chalcedony, which is also called the Speaker's Stone. Chalcedony also stands for reflection and meditation. What could be more useful in these hectic times.

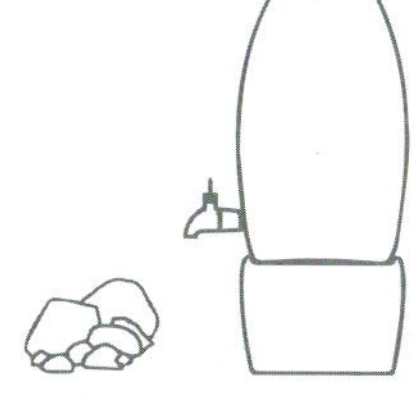

LOVE

GARNET

ROSE QUARTZ

CLEAR QUARTZ

PROPERTIES

All you need is ... water. And when you add rose quartz, the quintessential stone of love, tenderness and sensuality, anything is possible. Fair and lovely rose quartz is a talisman for relationships and is used in crystal healing to release emotional wounds and traumas and to bring peace and calm. Fiery Garnet adds a wonderful component of sensuality and passion to this blend. Combined, they create a unique emotional dynamic - LOVE. For those who love water, this is the perfect gift.

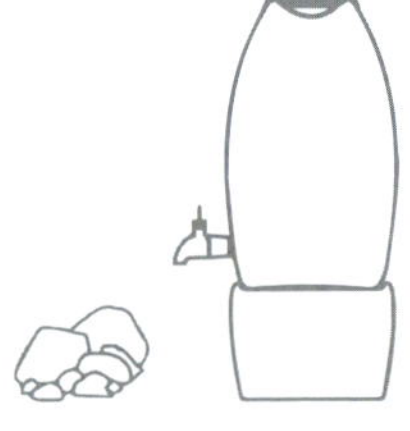

FOREVER YOUNG

AQUAMARINE

AVENTURINE

SMOKE QUARTZ

CLEAR QUARTZ

PROPERTIES

FOREVER YOUNG ... is designed to attract clarity, purity and fluidity like a natural mountain spring water on a crisp clear day. If your personal detox practices are important to you in these hectic times, the Forever Young blend offers an additional dimension of energetic cleansing. Aventurine has been used for regenerative purposes, aquamarine for cleansing and smoky quartz for stress relief. In the natural healing arts, this combination provides an invigorating cleanse of body and mind.

AYURVEDA

AMETHYST

MILK OPAL

CARNEALIAN

LAPIS LAZULI

GARNET

ORANGE CALCITE

CLEAR QUARTZ

PROPERTIES

The word Ayurveda means "science of life" and is the traditional holistic system of Indian medicine. The more than 3000-year-old concept also uses gems for therapeutic purposes. Ayurveda gem therapy claims that every gem has properties that can help to balance specific doshas and heal certain physical or emotional conditions. Experts helped us creating this blend with a focus on the seven basic Ayurvedic tissues.

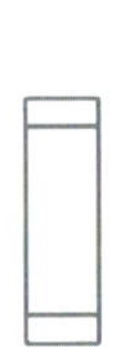

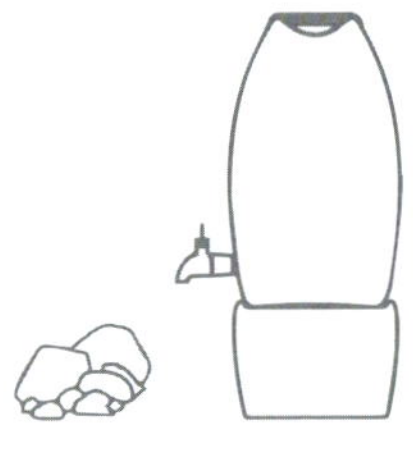

LUNA

MOONSTONE

CLEAR QUARTZ

PROPERTIES

LUNA ... is strongly connected to the energy of the moon, making it first and foremost, a women's stone. In traditional healing practices it is used to help strengthen a woman's intuitive sense, open the heart and to get in balance with the natural cycles of life. Wise women know about the effects of the moon on their body. Vibrating with the light of a full moon, rainbow moonstone provides a reflective, calming energy.

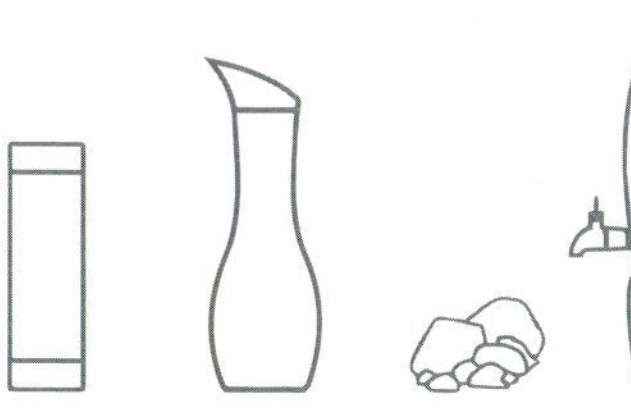

HAPPINESS

CARNEALIAN

NEPHRITE

ORANGE CALCITE

CLEAR QUARTZ

PROPERTIES

Natural healing traditions tell us this combination of beaming orange calcite and brilliant carnelian (the "Stone of Life") form a vibrant aura of openness, eloquence, and optimism. And to top it off, we've included beautiful jade. This "Dream Stone" is said to bless whatever it touches and has been famous over the last 6,000 years for attracting good luck.

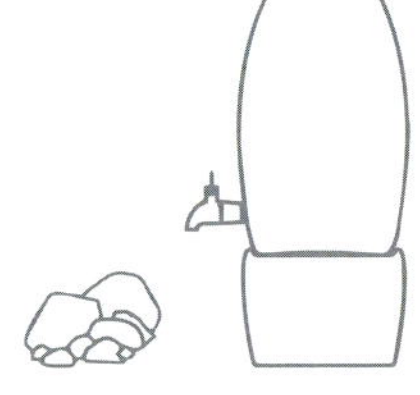

GUARDIAN

AMETHYST

TOURMALIN

CLEAR QUARTZ

PROPERTIES

New ideas, mental strength and inner growth require an open mind. This intense blend has been created to neutralize everything negative. In natural healing traditions, grounding black tourmaline stands for protection and safety. In several publications, Amethyst has been named the perfect companion for black tourmaline to create a powerful, natural shield against negativity. Clear Quartz adds a good portion of clarity.

INSPIRATION

LAPIS LAZULI

RUTILE QUARTZ

PROPERTIES

Change the world with your creativity and break fresh ground! Get inspired by enjoying a glass of crystal water from this enchanting combination of rutilated quartz and the deep, celestial blue lapis lazuli – a symbol for spirituality in ancient Egypt about 6,000 years ago. The beautiful, golden-streaked rutile is said to energize and to improve awareness. Feed your brainpower every day with this very special blend of gem water.

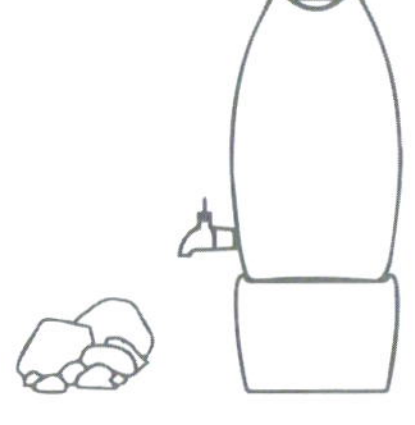

VITALITY

EMERALD

CLEAR QUARTZ

PROPERTIES

The 11th-century abbess Hildegard of Bingen wrote: The many green hughes of an emerald reflect the beautiful green colors of nature. Emerald is a crystal of the heart. It stands for renewal and regeneration like no other. This lush "growth crystal" has been a source of fascination in several cultures for over six thousand years and was considered a symbol of eternal life in ancient Egypt. Many believe emerald to have rejuvenating and restoring effects.

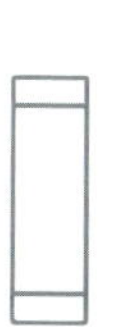 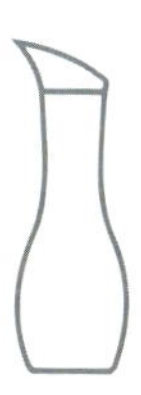    

DIAMOND

DIAMOND

CLEAR QUARTZ

PROPERTIES

Diamonds were already revered in ancient times as the kings of all gemstones. It was said to give its owner "divine splendor, supreme purity and enlightenment". The unique combination of diamond and Clear Quartz creates a source of power that eclipses anything previously associated with water. The clarity and purity of both gemstones amplify into an indomitable quest for spiritual freedom. No more lazy compromises, towards a permanent internal order. Diamond helps with strokes and heart attacks or similar circulatory diseases.

HERO

GOLD

TIGER EYE

SMOKE QUARTZ

CLEAR QUARTZ

PROPERTIES

The Hero blend implies courage, self-confidence, determination and fearlessness in its very name. With 24-karat gold leaf, tiger eye, smoky quartz and clear quartz, this blend is full of irrepressible energy. A truly animalistic combination combines all the attributes that everyday heroes need: Determination, alertness and a sense of opportunity.

GRATITUDE

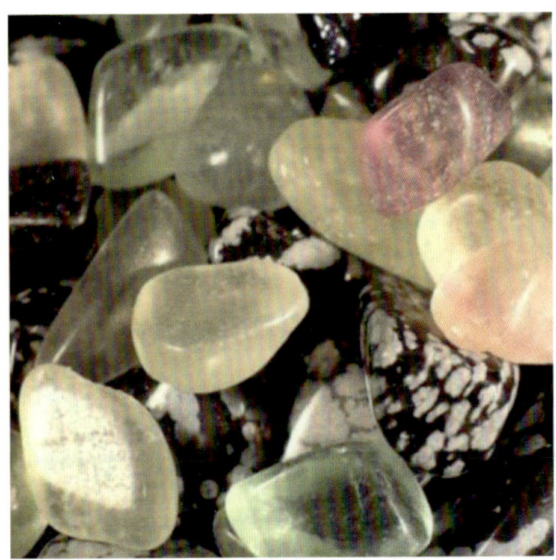

FLUORITE

SNOWFLAKE OBSIDIAN

PROPERTIES

Gratitude often makes one aware of the possibilities and opportunities we have been given. Through gratitude we see all the things that make our lives happier. Drink the water and contemplate the beauty of the stones that symbolize all the things that enrich our lives. Obsidian with snowflake inclusions leads us to a conscious, strong feeling of gratitude. Fluorite, one of the most powerful healing stones, has a physically and mentally liberating effect and stimulates new patterns of thought and behavior. Consider your current situation as a gift and look optimistically and confidently into the future.

SERENITY & FORGIVENESS

DUMORTIERITE

RHODONITE

PROPERTIES

Forgiveness is the most beautiful gift we can give ourselves. Free yourself from inner harm and hatred, live free and carefree again. Unburden your soul and rejoice with many friends around you. Dumortierite strengthens confidence in one's own greatness, makes one more tolerant and promotes a positive, serene attitude to life. Rhodonite enhances this effect, it is a gemstone for reconciliation, understanding and prudence.

TAKE IT EASY

DUMORTIERITE

CITRINE

CLEAR QUARTZ

PROPERTIES

How often do worries and fears dominate our thinking and block us? Studies have proven that 80 percent of all worries are unfounded or not true. Citrine increases the joy of life, helps with stress and anxiety. It is a pick-me-up and prevents worries from arising. Dumortierite creates confidence in one's own greatness, makes one more tolerant and promotes a positive, serene attitude towards life. This blend thus supports a carefree life.

SELF-AWARENESS

ORANGE CALCITE

JADE

PROPERTIES

This gemstone blend brings the ego back into balance, because this water promotes "self-awareness". With a new self-esteem towards a new future without fear, experience life with courage and enthusiasm. Orange calcite and jade in crystal water promote a unique radiance and are a source of increased self-awareness, inner balance, courage and confidence.

OPTIMISM

CARNEALIAN

MOSS AGATE

PROPERTIES

It is often an art to take life more lightly, to look forward with elation and enthusiasm. Carnelian motivates one with the drive and enthusiasm to tackle the future. Troubles are overcome, courage and steadfastness make everything easier. The moss agate separates us from old ties and constraints, and makes us look forward with confidence, inspired by new ideas. We leave fears, burdens and mental pressures behind us and look to an optimistic future.

BONES & JOINTS

ORANGE CALCITE

FLUORITE

PROPERTIES

Water transports important nutrients to our joints and bones, and it disposes of toxins and waste from our bodies. Our bones consist of 80 percent water and should remain flexible and supple well into old age. Fluorite strengthens joints, teeth and bones. At the same time, it builds up nerves, stimulates concentration and receptivity. Orange calcite stimulates metabolism and promotes the healing of tendons and bones. It is also a mood booster, making you optimistic and confident. This water is very suitable for the elderly and people who practice sports.

INNER STRENGTH & LEADERSHIP QUALITIE

CITRINE

AQUAMARINE

CLEAR QUARTZ

PROPERTIES

A strong personality is characterized by a clear view and inner strength. One's own viewpoints are presented with confident demeanor. The citrine reinforces these qualities. It is a clarifying stone that helps goal-oriented and determined people find their career path and take leadership. Aquamarine not only gives foresight and prudence, but also perseverance to achieve set goals.

THINK POSITIVE

CARNEALIAN

GARNET

CLEAR QUARTZ

PROPERTIES

The world belongs to the happy one. A positive outlook on life not only promotes physical attributes such as strong immunity, it opens doors, encourages successful communication and brings new, positive friends. Carnelian gives a more optimistic outlook to see life from a joyful point of view. Garnet promotes a zest for life, helps against melancholy and depression, makes fun-loving and confident. If you drink this blend, you will find that the world smiles at you and a lot of things become easier.

BODY & SOUL

ROSE QUARTZ

SAPPHIRE

CLEAR QUARTZ

PROPERTIES

Feeling good always has to do with a healthy body, high self-esteem and a good balance of body and soul. Rose quartz makes receptive to the beauty in life, for pleasure, sensuality and aesthetics. Sapphire helps one with introspection, to become aware of one's own beauty. It supports self-forgiveness and stimulates self-love. This blend takes away public anxiety and gives a confident appearance even in a crowd.

INTIMACY

MALACHITE

GOLD

CLEAR QUARTZ

PROPERTIES

There is no alternative to an intimate togetherness, a deep connection. Security, trust, affection, love gives solid strength to a couple's relationship. Gold is most often chosen for wedding rings - nothing symbolizes the extraordinary union of two people better than this rare metal. Malachite inspires love for a loved one and strengthens affection and trust for a harmonious partnership. Cuddle together and drink together from a glass with this mixture - this is heaven on earth.

INDIVIDUAL
CRYSTAL WATER

The concept is unique. Use a powerful and energetic clear quartz and put about 70 grams in the lower gemstone depot of the bottle. Voilà, your own crystal water is ready. Why clear quartz? Because it is not only a very powerful stone, but especially because it enhances the effect of all other gemstones. Furthermore, you can add another stone or more, depending on the effect or tendency, in the depot. This way you can quickly make your own individual crystal water.

If you want a change, you can fill the bottle with your own favorite stones. Of course, the gemstones can be changed depending on the situation.

The bottle has a separate compartment, the so-called gemstone depot, in which you can put the stones, so they do not come into direct contact with the drinking water. This ensures that neither impurities nor toxins of the stones are ingested along with the water. Only the information from the stones will flow into the drink.

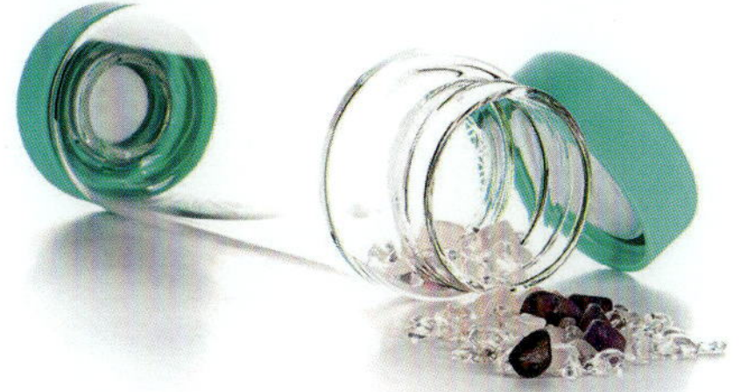

With this bottle, your own individuality can be given unlimited space. They are perfect for personal crystal healing therapy, both physical and spiritual. Also, the preference for crystal water of a particular stone, its color, effect, etc., can be realized with this bottle.

At the same time, you can give more power and expression to your own zodiac sign with the corresponding gemstone.

The significant gemstones for each zodiac sign are:

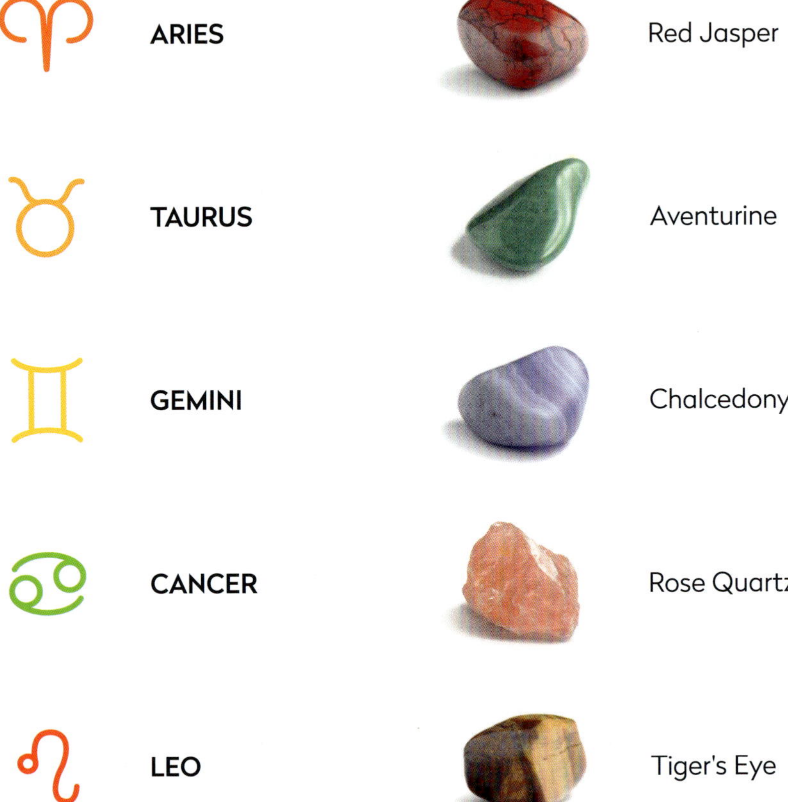

ARIES		Red Jasper
TAURUS		Aventurine
GEMINI		Chalcedony
CANCER		Rose Quartz
LEO		Tiger's Eye

 **VIRGO**  Carnelian

 **LIBRA**  Serpentine

 **SCORPIUS**  Obsidian

 **SAGITTARIUS**  Sodalite

 **CAPRICORNUS**  Amethyst

 **AQUARIS**  Fluorite

 **PISCES**  Agate

GEMSTONE BLENDS
FOR INU BOTTLES

SEVEN CHAKRAS
ACCESS ALL YOUR INNER RESOURCES

AMETHYST, SODALITE, ROSE QUARTZ, PERIDOT
CARNELIAN, GARNET, CLEAR QUARTZ

This colorful gemstone blend includes a matching stone for each of the main energy centers, called chakras. The chakras are considered the connection point to the universal energy of life and thus influence our general well-being. Conscious breathing exercises in yoga and meditation help to open these energy centers. The right framework for this is provided by a healthy diet and sufficient fresh and living crystal water.

YIN YANG

BOTH SIDES OF LIFE

BLACK TOURMALINE, MILK OPAL, CLEAR QUARTZ

In Chinese philosophy, yin and yang stand for opposing forces that do not fight each other, but rather are mutually dependent. Without Yin there is no Yang and vice versa. If the two forces are in balance, the energies can flow freely. Black tourmaline and white milk opal uniquely embody the principle of yin and yang, informing water with the perfect energy of day and night, movement and stillness, adventurousness and reservation.

LOVE
LOVE IS ALL AROUND

ROSE QUARTZ

Love is the highest energy in the universe and the most beautiful feeling that can infuse us. This energy and feeling is ideally embodied in rose quartz. Rose quartz is the stone of harmony and sensitivity. It is said that it can also eliminate relationship fears and worries and stimulate a spiritual connection with your partner. Perfect against heartbreak!

VISION
VISIONS RESULT IN ASTONISHING ACHIEVEMENTS

NOBLE SHUNGITE, AQUAMARINE, CLEAR QUARTZ

Where would we be without visions? And what good would these do us if we did not try to implement them with all our might? The mixture helps to follow the longing, to realize goals and not to let anyone stop you. The VISION gemstone blend revitalizes drinking water in a unique way and provides the body with the best water every day. The protective effect of noble shungite and the positive energy of aquamarine in terms of vision, dynamism and endurance can be felt.

AMBER
THE LIGHTNESS OF BEING

AMBER, CLEAR QUARTZ

There is much more to amber, widely known as jewelry, than meets the eye. In gemstone healing, it is especially valued for its positive effect on our mind. It provides harmony and self-confidence, communicates sociability and spontaneity. Amber and clear quartz give the drinking water incomparable lightness and freshness. What better way to start the day than with a bottle full of happiness!

LARIMAR

BOUNDLESS LIVELINESS

LARIMAR, CLEAR QUARTZ

Exclusively mined in the Dominican Republic, Larimar appears like a glimpse into the soul of the Caribbean. Turquoise blue, offset with a network of fine white lines, it is undeniable. It conveys inner peace and has an inspiring effect. By doing so, it allows us to see new perspectives and encourages us to take our lives into our own hands. With this blend you can enjoy the pure freshness and liveliness of an extraordinary jewel.

ORIGINS - AUSTRALIA
VITALIZE YOUR SENSES

MOOKAIT

The energy of gemstones is forever associated with the special atmosphere of their origin. Australia, this continent stands first and foremost for untouched vastness, adventure and originality, it is also the home of the Mookait. Named after its place of discovery, Mooka Creek in Western Australia, its name means "flowing water" among the Aborigines. With this water you can feel the energy of these original places, they help for a little time-out with magical moments full of exoticism and energy. At the same time, it awakens the joy of movement and a sense of adventure. A faithful companion for all who want to go new ways without forgetting your roots.

CRYSTAL WATER
THE DRINK
OF THE FUTURE

Whether an innovation is accepted by civilization often depends not on its ingenuity, but on whether this invention is also accompanied by an improvement in old methods and a change in rigid patterns of thought; it becomes common knowledge when an elementary benefit is created. Here's an example: In the early 17th century, Europeans increasingly used a fork, but this was initially considered silly. Today, eating with a knife and fork is the essence of modern Western food culture.

Water is the most important element for humans. Water is life - healthy water is healthy life. Nothing influences our organism more than the quality of the water we drink. More and more people are wondering today whether water should continue to be made drinkable with chemical additives or whether the natural energy of precious stones can achieve the same effect.

Fresh, healthy spring water also flows over stones that have had a consistently high energetic quality for millions of years. As in many areas of life, a return to the resources of nature is about to begin.

Some inventions, in retrospect, were the impulse for the beginning of a new era, because new ways of thinking accelerated the development of mankind. For me, it is only logical that crystal water will become more and more important in all households in the future. Simply because it tastes better and works at the same time. Even if the connections behind it cannot yet be fully explained by science - like infinitely many other phenomena that exist on our planet.

CRYSTAL WATER CONVINCES THROUGH TASTE AND EFFECT.

DR. PETER KASTNER

As a medical doctor, I am of course aware of the enormous influence water has on my body and my health. For more than 25nyears I have been using various reverse osmosis systems. When I then observed in animals how almost greedily they drank gemstone water and I could also see positive effects, it was natural for me to drink gemstone water myself.

Every time I look at a shelf in my basement, I realize how much money I've spent on things in my life that were important to me in the past and now become almost forgotten in this shelf, sitting there because I could decide whether to dispose of them or not.
On the other hand, there are things that I've been using every day for years with the same enthusiasm as my gemstone water. I exclusively use crystal water to rinse my nose in the morning. The beautifully designed gemstone vessels enhance the ambience in my living environment and greatly add to my well-being. I enjoy it daily to choose between the different gem mixes.

If there's one thing for me that never becomes banal, it's drinking gem water. Gemstone water does not only promote my health and that of my family, but it enriches my whole life.

Peter Kastner

DR. GABNUS IHEANACHO OKAFOR

Dear Ewald Eisen,
my name is Gabi Okafor and I live in Lagos, Nigeria. I am a practicing doctor and trainer for authentic, living biological methods of curing diseases.

My healing principle is based on creating an environment that allows the body to heal conditions themselves, both internally and externally. I make use of natural systems and biotechnologies to activate the dynamics and restore the balance of the wisdom of our own body. My focus is a holistic approach for everybody. Your concept of living water is a vital part of this.

Many thanks to you, Ewald, for helping the world by inventing health-promoting water knowledge with so much love and in such an excellent way. I congratulate you and your mission, to raise global awareness for the importance of drinking healthy and living water. This is of elemental importance in a world where most of the available water is biologically dead.

I applied your method on myself and on my patients with astonishing success. Thank you again for your pioneering idea. I'm sure she will conquer the world.

Sincerely, Gabi Okafor

SUMMARY

Nature is the most powerful institution on Earth. Everybody is taking about sustainability these days. Everything we look for related to sustainability in our lifestyle is something we can easily find in nature.

PAGES 8-21

Nature doesn't need us, but we need nature.

Everything we invent and develop to simulate nature isn't nearly as genial as nature itself.

There are countless man-made treatment plants, but none of them compare to nature's congenial way to create healthy and vital water like fresh from a spring.

Nature will always strike back when we act against it.

When we act against nature, in the end we act against ourselves.

Shaping water with information

PAGES 52-57

There is no medium that is so "thirsty' for information like water.

Water processes information by forming clusters with its oxyen- and hydrogen molecules. Those clusters pass on the information to our cells.

Information can be shaped negatively (sickness) or positively (health).

**Water is our most important food,
essential for a healthy live.**

PAGES 86-100

70% of our body cells is water.

Healthy water makes our cells stronger, healthier and more robust.

With a healing potential of 70% nothing impacts our health more than water.

Our current attitude towards water

We perceive water as nothing special, even as boring.

To us, water seems to be available everywhere and all of the time. We don't have to fight for water (yet).

We use water for all kinds of things.

It's translucent, has no taste or smell.

We usually don't feel an immediate impact by drinking contaminated water. Most pollutions are subtle and have a long-term effect on our body.

Our NEW attitude towards water

PAGES 104 - 115

The famous pioneer in water research, Masaru Emoto, found out that 50% of the effect of water is determined by its quality, and the 50% by our attitude towards water.

Drink water with the intention of healing and well-being.

Imagine how water heals and strengthens your cells with every sip.

Drinking water when we are thirsty leads to a undersupply of water in our body. Like driving a car on fuel reserve and then refueling just a little bit.

Drinking 30 ml (1 fl.oz.) per kilogram (2.2 lbs.) every day provides for a sufficient supply of water.

The perfect moto: Love what you drink!

The best water

PAGES 116-123

Nature shows us that stones are the key to vital water.
Primal element stone vitalizes primal element water.
Stones shape the best water with subtle vibrations.

PAGES 124-212

Every stone has its own frequency, thus having a unique effect.

PAGES 220-235

Crystal water is the best, healthiest water with a quality like water from a natural spring.

Precious stones create precious water with exceptional vitality. People drinking crystal water report that they love the taste and the incredible increase in well-being and life quality.

PAGE 300

Dr. Peter Kastner: „If there's anything that I'll never find banal, it's drinking crystal water. It keeps me and my family healthy and enrichens my life."

„Crystal water is the first choice for our health and our well-being. It provides for a long and active live. It tastes great and it works!."

Ewald Eisen

SOURCES

Of course, I have acquired this great specialized knowledge only from conversations with scientist friends, seminars or from publications.

To be mentioned are:

My friends:

Masaru Emoto
Michael Gienger
Monika Grundmann
Walter von Holst
Peter Lind
Marco Schreier

My main publications:

Hendel, Barbara and Ferreira, Peter:
Water and Salt, Herrsching 2001

Emoto, Masaru:
Hidden Messages in Water, Dorfen 2010

Pollack, Gerald H.:
Water, much more than H2O, Kirchzarten 2014

Holst, Walter von and Kühni, Werner:
Encyclopedia of Crystal Healing, Aarau 2003

Holst, Walter von and Kühni, Werner:
Healthy through healing crystals and oils, Aarau 2005

Gienger, Michael and Goebel, Joachim:
Gem Water. Production - Application - Effect, Saarbrücken 2006

Gienger, Michael:
Healing Crystals. The A–Z Guide to 555 Gemstones,
Baden-Baden 2014

Gienger, Michael:
Encyclopedia of Healing Stones. From Agate to Zoisite,
Saarbrücken 1997

My most important websites:

www.edelsteine.net
www.energymuse.com
www.heilsteine-ratgeber.net
www.heilsteinwiki.de
www.marcoschreier.de
www.steinheilkunde-ev.de
www.ruebe-zahl.de

www.vitajuwel.com

**Further
information**

Having been involved with these topics for over 40 years myself, I know how much work, time and passion is behind all this knowledge. Therefore, I would like to thank all my teachers and friends and the afore mentioned authors from the bottom of my heart for all their wonderful insights and wish them a precious and happy life.

Ewald Eisen